Translating Strategy INTO Shareholder Value

Translating Strategy into Shareholder Value

A COMPANY-WIDE APPROACH TO VALUE CREATION

RAYMOND J. TROTTA

AMACOM

American Management Association

New York • Atlanta • Brussels • Chicago • Mexico City • San Francisco
Shanghai • Tokyo • Toronto • Washington, D.C.

Special discounts on bulk quantities of AMACOM books are available to corporations, professional associations, and other organizations. For details, contact Special Sales Department, AMACOM, a division of American Management Association, 1601 Broadway, New York, NY 10019.
Tel.: 212-903-8316. Fax: 212-903-8083.
Web site: www.amacombooks.org

This publication is designed to provide accurate and authoritative information in regard to the subject matter covered. It is sold with the understanding that the publisher is not engaged in rendering legal, accounting, or other professional service. If legal advice or other expert assistance is required, the services of a competent professional person should be sought.

Library of Congress Cataloging-in-Publication Data

Trotta, Raymond J.
Translating strategy into shareholder value : a company-wide approach to value creation / Raymond J. Trotta.
    p.   cm.
Includes bibliographical references and index.
ISBN 0-8144-0564-9
    1. Corporations—Valuation.   2. Corporations—Finance.
3. Value.   I. Title.

HG4028.V3T76   2003
658.15—dc21

                                                    2003005479

Printing number

10   9   8   7   6   5   4   3   2   1

To my parents for their dedication and resolve
To Sherry Trotta, my wife, for her motivation and
support throughout this effort.
To Father Sabas Kilian, deceased professor of
Fordham University, whose inspiration drove the
actuation of our ideas.

Contents

Preface

STRATEGY deals with creating a sustainable competitive advantage for a business. The focus of business strategy is traditionally long-term in nature and is primarily concerned with the longevity of the business. Finance, on the other hand, is concerned with making management decisions in order to achieve its objective of increasing wealth for its owners. Finance looks at ways to obtain, manage, and utilize funds for wealth maximization. The two disciplines are many times perceived as working against each other. Yet, business leaders know that firms that have a sustainable competitive advantage become more valuable than their competition.

I have focused on the problem of aligning strategy with value creation for many years—as a management consultant serving global clients. The conceptual inspiration for this work can be traced to 1997, when I met Jim Hudick, who was the Global Practice Leader in Finance for the American Management Association (a worldwide management training organization). Jim contributed his thoughts around the conceptual framework and the notion of an economic filter, as well as the initial draft of the introduction and preface of this book.

During Jim's tenure at the AMA, we joined forces to develop a new management-training seminar. In that seminar, we presented the financial and economic aspects of corporate strategy as a critical step for the creation of shareholder value. Subsequently, we also worked together on a special conference entitled *"Partnering to Create Shareholder Value"* held in Newport Beach, February 2001. This book is an outgrowth of those earlier works. The focus of this effort is on "shareholder value creation," which is the central business issue confronting organizations. All businesses have a common goal—to increase in shareholder value. Nevertheless, many companies do not link strategy and finance in a concerted effort to achieve strategic goals. There is a disconnect between functional disciplines within the corporate architecture and an organizational obstacle that needs to be overcome. This disconnect has been recognized by numerous academic organizations. "We're trying to prepare people to appreciate that technical silos are not very effective in the workplace."[1]

I intend to continue this essential integration of disciplines by increasing an understanding of the interrelationship of finance, strategy, and value creation. One of the biggest challenges in business is to create a collective approach between the various functions of the business. I am writing this book to

bridge the gap between strategy and finance. Strate-
gists are proactively shaping the future of the business to assure its long-term dominance. Meanwhile,
financial analysts are quantitatively measuring (and
controlling) the results of these plans on a current/
short-term perspective versus budget.

I will help to bridge the gaps and resolve the con-
flicts that exist between the functional disciplines (as
described above). All sides can gain from this book
because it builds a bridge between vision (strategy)
and value creation (shareholder wealth). The development and implementation of strategy to create
shareholder value must be a team effort. All disciplines must partner together to achieve a common
goal—creating shareholder value. Financial techniques serve as a method of validation that business
strategy is creating shareholder value and not as an
end in itself. "The whole idea is that CFOs pushing
buttons to create shareholder value is an abstraction
from reality if they don't have a feel for marketing
strategies, and don't develop financial strategies that
make sense to the other side of the house."[2]

This book is a must-read for all businesspeople
regardless of discipline. The book is intended for
every businessperson who wants a practical, grass-
roots method of how to assess the alignment between
strategy and shareholder value. My purpose is to provide businesspeople (and students) with a basic understanding of how business strategy translates into

shareholder value. I will focus on the financial and economic assessment of strategy as a means for value creation using a step-wise approach.

This book is for businesspeople of all backgrounds—both financial and nonfinancial—at all levels of the organization. Just about every decision maker in business can benefit from the principles we will present. I will attempt to explain complex ideas in simple terms using easy-to-understand examples. I will provide readers with concepts and frameworks that can help create a collaborative approach to shaping strategy across all executive and operational functions throughout their organizations. In addition, this book provides a perspective required for corporate advancement. A critical competency of a senior manager is to understand how to translate strategy into the bottom line. After reading this book, the reader will have a better capability to:

- ❒ Understand the impact of economic conditions and market (industry) forces on his business.

- ❒ Assess the financial repercussions of strategy.

- ❒ Identify and assess Strategic Alternatives.

- ❒ Evaluate Strategic Alternatives within the context of fluid business conditions.

Notes

1. *CFO,* April 1997.
2. Ibid.

Acknowledgments

Creative Advice
Christopher Gardner—iValue
James P. Hudick—Institute of Management Accountants
Douglas Jones—Arbella Insurance Company

Research and Administrative Team
John Fischer
Christina Rocco
James Stephanou
Kelsey Trotta
Virginia Trotta

Reviewers

Blake Hill Ph.D.	Johns Hopkins University
Toni Lesowitz Ph.D.	LGI Group
Thomas Macfadden	Thomas Macfadden & Associates
Gary Raczek	MB Financial

Introduction

THIS BOOK links strategy and finance through a Step-Wise Approach to Value (SWAV). The Step-Wise Approach to Value is an analytical framework that combines strategic and financial analysis to evaluate Strategic Alternatives. The framework is conceptual in nature, so it has the flexibility to accommodate different types of cases. A Strategic Alternative (SA) is defined as an initiative that is implemented to increase shareholder value. The central premise of the SWAV is that the effectiveness of business strategy is validated through the creation of shareholder value.

This work follows the analytical flow of the SWAV, as illustrated in Exhibit I-1. It is similar to a funnel because it becomes increasingly more difficult to pass through the filters. I will first examine how value is created. I will look at the following strategic alternatives: mergers and acquisitions, technology, re-engineering, and outsourcing.

I will then discuss tools that are used in each filter. The goal is to develop a conceptual understanding of these analytical tools and how they are applied. The Step-Wise Approach to Value applies four filters, or screens, to assess the creation of shareholder value. The filters are designed to eliminate the Strategic Alternatives that do not have the prospect of creating shareholder value. As each filter is applied to an SA, one makes a decision to subject the Strategic Alternative to the tests in the next filter, or to remove it from consideration. A side benefit of SWAV is that it facilitates the planning process by continually focusing the planning group on viable alternatives.

What are the four filters in the SWAV framework? They are:

1. The economic filter

2. The strategic filter

3. The operational filter

4. The valuation filter

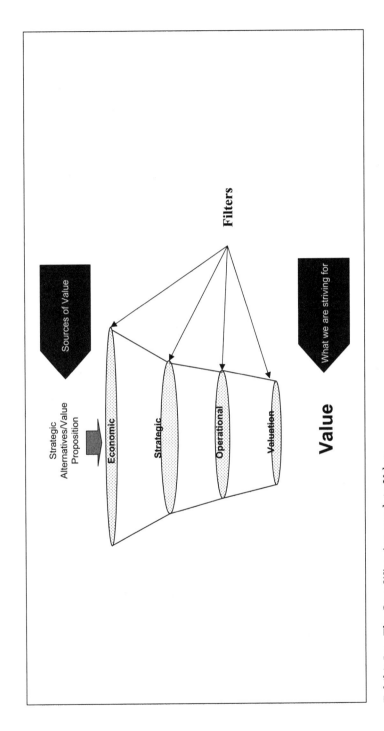

Exhibit I-1. The Step-Wise Approach to Value.

The Economic Filter

The economic and strategic filters take a macro view, which is a high-level assessment of a Strategic Alternative. These aspects of the SWAV involve analysis based on trends in the economy and industry.

Economic factors play a significant role in the successes and failures of businesses. In the case of large companies, value is tightly linked to the performance of the economy. As a company grows to Fortune 1000 proportions, this relationship increases in strength. Revenues, profits, and value tend to move in lockstep with economic conditions. This filter looks at key economic drivers and their impact on market demand. Our definition of market demand is simply:

Product Price $\times$ Number of Buyers = Market Demand.

Based on market demand for a product or service, you can understand whether the Strategic Alternative will create or destroy shareholder value. This economic filter tests the alignment of the SA with the direction of market demand.

The Strategic Filter

The strategic filter looks at how Strategic Alternatives impact your company's competitive advantage. This can be done in two ways. The first is by using the Porter Model. This involves framing the industry landscape in the context of five forces that shape industry change. I will describe how to discern your position in the value chain. Then I will help you to identify weaknesses in your current strategy.

The second is the Balanced Scorecard. This tool brings nonfinancial metrics into the managerial tool kit. I will describe how the Balanced Scorecard can be used to assess your strategy. It can be used as a tool for addressing critical success factors across four perspectives: financial (satisfying your shareholders), customer, internal business process, and ability to change and improve (learning and growth).

With the results from the analysis using the Porter Model and the Balanced Scorecard, you can determine whether the SA creates value by improving competitive advantage.

The Operational Filter

Now that we've tested the Strategic Alternative with the economic and strategic filters, we move to the operational aspect of the SWAV. A number of tools are used to analyze financial performance. Measurement of management performance (using the DuPont Model) and value creation using intrinsic value models (discounted cash flow analyses) will be demonstrated.

The drives of shareholder returns: profit margins, efficient utilization of assets, and leverage are then presented. How to assess your management of 1) the income statement to increase cash flow and 2) the balance sheet to increase asset turnover (utilization of assets) will be illustrated. By understanding these tools you will be in a position to increase return on assets. This discussion will also show you how the use of leverage (change in the amount of debt used to finance corporate investments) can help to further optimize return to shareholders.

The use of activity-based costing to obtain meaningful information for decision making will be described. Most financial reporting systems and standard costing systems simply don't do the job, particularly in today's competitive environment. They look backward and are general ledger and transaction–orientated. Accordingly, focus will be on the application of ABC/ABM Models to quantify resources consumed and the real cost of each activity. ABC (activity-based costing) models help businesses understand the true costs of doing business. ABM (activity-based management) models are systems that use ABC techniques to help managers improve the financial performance of their businesses by identifying ways to reduce the costs to production, customer service, and sales channels. I will also look at the estimation of the true costs of production and determination of real, measurable benefits.

Examination of operational drivers is key in addressing both short- and long-term impacts of Strategic Alternatives on shareholder value.

The Valuation Filter

Here, a guide to the analytics necessary to test how future strategy creates value is provided. The starting point is the use of statistics and regression methods to facilitate strategic planning and forecasting. An ability to model and forecast key business drivers is important. Intrinsic value techniques are utilized to estimate future financial results. Ability to consistently achieve sustainable growth rates and still maintain a positive financial spread over the cost of equity is a key factor for future success.

Dealing with uncertainty poses special problems requiring sophisticated financial forecasting techniques. Simulation models refine the inputs to shareholder value analysis.

The outcome of this filter is to determine if the Strategic Alternative creates shareholder value. Shareholder value is created when there is an increase in intrinsic value. "Intrinsic or estimated value is the present value of the expected cash flows from that asset."[1]

Now that an analytical arsenal has been built, we offer our final thoughts on the deployment of the approach in the business environment. Change is invariably meet with resistance. The barriers that may be encountered in implementation of analytical and quantitative systems from consulting experience are delineated here. These will prove helpful as you migrate your organization to a value-based company.

This work is not intended to be an exhaustive in nature. Our objective is to provide the reader with an approach to bridge the gap between strategy and shareholder value that has been tested in client settings. New tools are continually introduced into the marketplace, and there are other Strategic Alternatives that companies can use to increase value. This book provides a foundation from which new strategic and financial innovations can be added.

Note

1. Charles P. Jones, *Investments: Analysis and Management,* 7th ed. (New York: John Wiley & Sons, 2000), p. 198.

PART 1

Introduction to Strategic Alternatives

CHAPTER 1

Value and Value Proposition

THE STEP-WISE Approach to Value (SWAV) is a method to assess the value derived from a Strategic Alternative (SA). Following the path illustrated in Exhibit 1-1, we need to understand what we are looking for (shareholder value) and how it is generated (value proposition) before discussing the value filters. This chapter will deal with the concept of value; more specifically, what it is and how it is derived.

Value has become a buzzword. We constantly hear executives say things like:

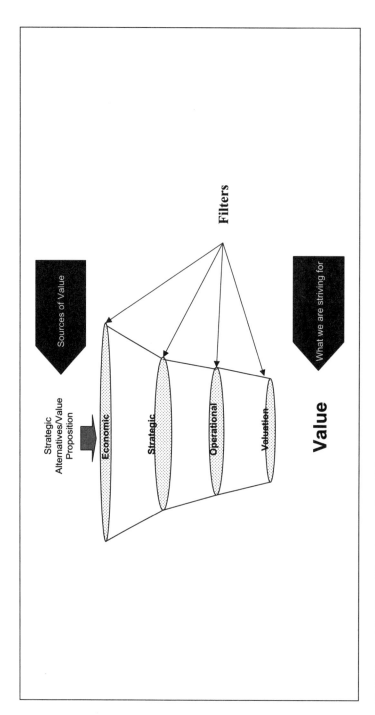

Exhibit 1-1. The Step-Wise Approach to Value.

Book Value
Total Assets
Less: Depreciation and Amortization
Equals
Net Assets
Less: Liabilities
Equals
Book Value

Year	Book Value (1)	Market Value (2)	Surplus over Book Value	Distortion (3)
Purchase	$1,000,000	$1,000,000	Same	None
1	$970,000	$1,000,000	$30,000	3%
2	$940,000	$1,030,000	$90,000	9%
3	$910,000	$1,060,900	$150,900	14%
4	$880,000	$1,092,727	$212,727	19%
5	$850,000	$1,125,509	$275,509	24%
6	$820,000	$1,159,274	$339,274	29%
7	$790,000	$1,194,052	$404,052	34%
8	$760,000	$1,229,874	$469,874	38%
9	$730,000	$1,266,770	$536,770	42%
10	$700,000	$1,304,773	$604,773	46%

(1) Depreciation over 30 years ($30,000 per year) with a $100,000 salvage value
(2) Appreciation rate of 3% per year
(3) Surplus divided by market value

Exhibit 1-2. Book value.

to allow for wear and tear. For example, assume you had a commercial building that was purchased for $1 million and it was depreciated over a thirty-year period, a salvage value of $100,000. Now suppose that the market price of the building increases at a rate of 3 percent per year. The amount of cash the property could be sold for may be rising, and the book value could be falling, as also illustrated in Exhibit 1-2. Over a ten-year period the distortion in value (surplus over book value divided by market value) grows to 46 percent of market value (Exhibit 1-3).

The next issue is that the book value method is based on historic transactions. The value of the building on the books is determined by what the company paid for the property less depreciation (adjustments may be made for improvements over time). The problem is that book value does not look at future growth in value based on changes in demand and the receipt of future cash streams.

Market Value

Market value is the price at which buyers and sellers trade similar items in an open marketplace. In the absence of a market price, market value is the estimated highest price a buyer would be warranted in paying and a seller justified in accepting, provided both parties were fully informed and acting intelligently and

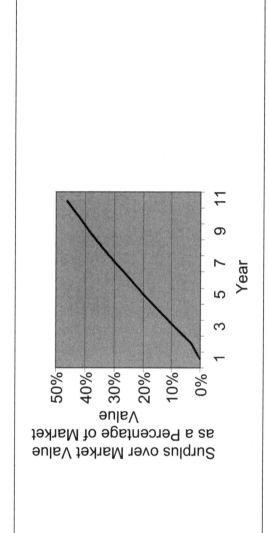

Exhibit 1-3. Value distortion.

voluntarily. This is the price that a willing buyer and a willing seller would pay if the transaction would be consummated today or in the near future. The market value of a stock is what it is trading for today. The problem with this form of value is that it may be based on a "market bubble." Market bubbles are over-valuations in assets based on irrational behaviors of investors. For example, many Internet stocks in the late 1990s were overvalued based on hype in the business community. Technology analysts saw great growth in market demand for the Internet by consumers and businesses. The bubble did burst as the hype did not transform itself into reality. The ability of the Internet companies to generate cash was in many cases nonexistent.

Analysts have created ways to rationalize the future growth in terms of market price by using the earnings multipliers. They use the following formula to understand value:

Market Value = Earnings × Price/Earnings Multiplier

This equates the value of a company with its earnings and a multiplier. Another way to think about this formula is that the multiplier represents some premium that a buyer will pay over current earnings. The premium is in many respects an adjustment for the ability of a company to produce earnings and future growth. The major issue with the multiplier approach is that earnings are not a strong indicator of value and cash generation.

Intrinsic Value

We mentioned that intrinsic value is an estimate of value based on the present value of cash flows. In its simplest form an equation for intrinsic value is:

$$\text{Value} = \frac{\textit{Sum of Future Cash Flows}}{\text{Adjustment of Time and Risk}}$$

We will discuss the math behind intrinsic value in Chapter 11. Why is this superior to market and book value? Most importantly, the intrinsic value model is cash flow–based. Cash flow is defined as benefits less costs and taxes. Research has shown that the value of companies has a strong correlation to value.[1] This method is more conducive to analyzing SAs. Alternatives that involve changes to the way companies do business are difficult to value, based on market and book value concepts. Reengineering, for example, would most likely be accounted for as an operating expense and not an asset. Hence, a book value calculation could not be used. It would be difficult to find a market for a reengineering initiative because of the specialized and proprietary nature of this alternative.

In addition, the intrinsic value model is forward-looking. It focuses on future cash flows.

This valuation concept is not without weaknesses. If assumptions are performed incorrectly, such as in estimation of cash flows and time/risk adjustments, the quality of the analysis is just as flawed as the market and book value models. We will deal with the weaknesses and how to offset them in the section dedicated to discounted cash flow in Chapter 11. On the other hand, the intrinsic value model has the best fit for our purposes.

Understanding the Value Proposition: How Is Value Created?

With our objective defined (intrinsic value), we must focus on how to get there (value creation). Based on the SWAV, adding value would be increasing intrinsic value, which is increasing future cash flows. In the introduction to this chapter we mentioned hackneyed expressions like "adding value." The way SAs increase value is called the value proposition. The SWAV will test whether value propositions are increasing or adding value using the successively more stringent filters. There are three types of value propositions:

1. Revenue increase and maintenance (RIM)

2. Competitive repositioning

3. Efficiency

The goal is to turn these value propositions into a stream of cash. The objective of the SWAV is to increase the probability of creating a cash stream that will increase intrinsic value. Let's explore these value propositions in detail.

Revenue Increase and Maintenance

One aspect of this value proposition is in many respects self-explanatory. A Strategic Alternative will increase value if it generates cash from increasing revenue. The relationship is that rising revenue will drive increasing cash flow. The assumption here is that costs and taxes do not exceed the revenue boost. Increasing revenue becomes more difficult in established industries. This occurs because there is greater competition for the same dollar of revenue. This intense competition tends to drive down cash flow because of pricing pressures (see the Porter Model in Chapter 5). This value proposition is normally associated with mergers and acquisitions.

The maintenance aspect of the RIM value proposition is less intuitive. Revenue maintenance is thwarting the loss of revenue driven by market conditions. A company may invest in a technology initiative to improve customer retention. For example, computer telephony interface (CTI) technology improves the flow of information from core systems to the point of contact with the customer. The benefit is improved customer service through improved access to account information and less wait time. The key assumption here is that a Strategic Alternative will protect the existing stream of cash flow. The underlying premise is that revenue and hence cash flow will be lost if the investment is not made. Revenue maintenance investments are normally made if companies feel that they are catching up to their competition. In the CTI instance, the other competitors would already have this technology. The evaluating company would consider a CTI investment as a "strategic necessity." In the past, managers would use the strategic necessity argument to move forward with SAs that did not have strong quantitative support. With the analytical rigor of the SWAV, SAs will need to be validated through the generation of intrinsic value.

Competitive Repositioning

This is an increase in competitive position that results in increased intrinsic value. Competitive repositioning increases value through:

❏ Increasing or maintaining market share

❏ Improving competitive intelligence

❏ Differentiating the company from its competition

Increasing or Maintaining Market Share

The underlying assumption is that there is a direct relationship between market share and cash flow similar to RIM and cash flow. This assumption requires rigorous testing through the SWAV. There have been many mergers that were justified on increased market share that have destroyed value. Integration expenses reeled out of control and resulted in a future cash drain as opposed to an increase.

Improving Competitive Intelligence

Competitive intelligence is knowledge and/or information that gives a business a competitive advantage over its rivals. A competitive advantage is obtained by acquiring information about customers, suppliers, markets, and channels. (For instance, a point of sale capability that collects information on customer buying behaviors.) This type of information gives a company the ability to stock shelves with products that customers want. This type of intelligence gives a company an advantage over its competition because it has a better idea about what will sell. The key to this value proposition is that having the information does not necessarily mean that a company can use it to improve future cash flow.

Differentiating the Company from Its Competition

This aspect of repositioning assumes that cash flow will be improved by doing things differently. An example of differentiation is a company who makes an acquisition to obtain a proprietary business process that will improve cash flow.

The major issues that will be vetted in the SWAV for repositioning value propositions are their long-term orientation and difficulty of measurement. The time frame to realize benefits from realization is generally long-term. This means that the adjustment for time and risk discussed above will dramatically mitigate the intrinsic value of the cash flow stream created. In addition, the benefit stream from differentiation is hard to measure. It takes a great deal more effort to analyze and measure the increase in value from an SA than through an increase in revenue, or the next value proposition category efficiency.

Efficiency

Efficiency improves cash flow by performing business processes better, faster, or cheaper than the current operation. Doing things better results in superior quality, such as lower defects in manufacturing environments. In a service environment one result could be better customer service.

Performing business processes faster can refer to the time to make a car or to approve a loan. Doing things faster must result in consumption of less resources or a lift in revenue to improve cash flow. For example, a furniture company buys new equipment that reduces labor costs by cutting down the amount of time it takes to build a table. The important thing to remember is that reduced time does not necessarily reduce costs. An illustration on the revenue side is cutting product introduction time. Introducing products faster can improve cash flow by improving profitability (the difference between benefits and costs).

This value proposition can also be justified by reduction or avoidance of costs. Costs are defined as operating and investment costs. Operating costs are costs associated with the maintenance and operation of a business. These costs are generally referred to as expenses and are found on the income statement of a business. Cost of goods (raw materials), labor, and maintenance contracts are examples of operating costs. Investment costs are those that create assets. These costs are found on the balance sheets of businesses: capital expenditures (purchase of buildings and equipment), capitalized intangibles (purchase of software, goodwill, or patents), and working capital (inventory and accounts receivable). Value propositions centered on efficiency are easier to measure and to quantify than repositioning and RIM.

Conclusion

This chapter dealt with understanding value and value propositions. Three concepts of value were discussed: book value, market value, and intrinsic value. Shareholder value based on a book value convention is net asset value less liabilities. Shareholder value based on a market value concept is the price paid by a willing buyer and a willing seller. Intrinsic value is the sum of future cash flows adjusted for time and risk. We have chosen the intrinsic value method because it is cash flow–based, future-oriented, and accommodates the assessment of Strategic Alternatives.

The three main categories of value propositions are revenue increase and maintenance (RIM), competitive repositioning, and efficiency. RIM–related value propositions assume that increase or maintenance of revenue will have a similar impact on cash flow.

Competitive repositioning assumes that increased cash flow will be driven from increasing/maintaining market share, competitive intelligence, and differentiation. Efficiency assumes cash flow improvements from making business processes better, faster, or cheaper.

Note

1. McKinsey & Company, Inc., Tom Copeland, Tim Koller, and Jack Murrin, *Valuation: Measuring and Managing the Value of Companies,* 3rd ed. (New York: John Wiley & Sons, 2000), p. 77.

CHAPTER 2

External Strategic Alternatives

OUR OBJECTIVE in this chapter is to get a deeper understanding of external Strategic Alternatives. These are initiatives that involve tapping outside sources to increase value. Our focus will be on mergers and acquisitions (M&A) and outsourcing—two common external SAs that are prevalent and have questionable track records for success. One reason for the weak track record is the ill-formed linkage between the value proposition and shareholder value. The rationale for many mergers is predicated on "strategic reasons" that are not validated from a financial perspective. These strategic reasons tend to have a destructive influence on the business as a whole because the benefit streams are not adequately forecasted and the risks are not well articulated. Outsourcing alternatives are especially popular during economic downturns, but can trade short-term savings for long-term value. These arrangements tend to be used as a stopgap measure to satisfy short-term demands of institutional investors and industry analysts. They tend to be justified by short-term expense reduction. Outsourcing can be more expensive in the long run and create risks for the long-term viability of the business. Our focus will be on a description of these alternatives and the factors that determine success and failure—more specifically their rationale and risks. Let's begin by looking at M&A.

Mergers and Acquisitions

Business combinations and acquisitions are one of the most broadly used methods to execute strategy.

Mergerstat, an authority on M&A, tracks activity in this area. Their results over thirty years show increasing deal value (market value) over time (Exhibit 2-1). In addition, the number of mergers increased over time. There is a tendency for deal making to increase in times of economic expansion, both in num-

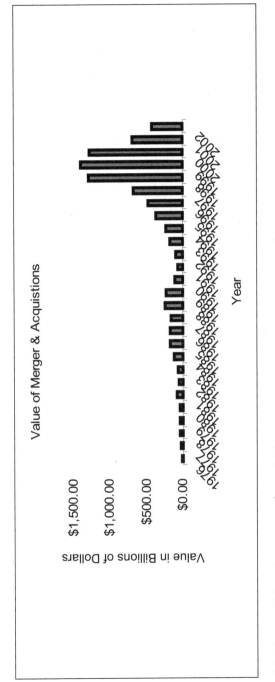

Exhibit 2-1. Value of mergers and acquisitions.

ber and in value. This is especially evident between 1994 and 1999. During recessionary periods activity tends to decline.

What are the implications of increasing deal value? The obvious conclusion to be drawn is that the sellers are getting wealthier. The seller's shareholders benefit from these price premiums, but the benefit to the acquiring company is not as clear. In a M&A strategy, the key question for the acquiring company is: How is shareholder value enhanced through buying companies? Let's look for answers in the rationale for mergers and acquisitions.

Rationale for Mergers and Acquisitions

Mergers and acquisitions can become extremely complex. Transactions require expertise from strategic, legal, financial, and operational disciplines to be successful. Each of these groups may have different criteria for success. There are many cases where deals are structured to hurdle tax and regulatory barriers. While these factors are beyond the scope of this book, it is important to understand that these issues introduce transactional complexities into the deal. Our view is purely strategic in nature, and our concern is limited to how mergers and acquisitions can deliver shareholder value through improving the strategy and operation of the business. To simplify the analysis,

M&A can be rationalized in three ways: 1) competitive integration, 2) supply chain movements, and 3) diversification.

Competitive Integration

Competitive integration occurs when companies in the same business—offering similar products and services to the same target market—combine. An example of this type was the merger of Daimler-Benz and Chrysler. Competitive integration mergers and acquisitions reduce the number of competitors in an industry. This increases the market position of the combined company. The primary strategic benefits of competitive integration are increased size, creating the perception that a company has a greater market presence (market share), superior resources, and improved economies of scale. As enterprises grow in size through this strategy, other competitors will seek to combine driven by growing sense of competitive weakness. The underlying assumption is that bigger is better. This type of thought process has led to a tremendous change in the banking industry as reflected in this excerpt from the Federal Reserve Bulletin on "Profits and balance sheet developments at U.S. commercial banks in 1998":

> Bank consolidation continued and included some particularly large mergers.

As a result, the share of industry assets at the largest one hundred banks rose to 70 percent at year end, up from 67$^{3}/_{4}$ percent a year earlier and around 50 percent in 1985. The number of commercial banks fell by 371, as the number of newly created banks was more than offset by the 588 banks that ceased to exist [almost entirely because of mergers]. At the end of 1998, there were 8,817 commercial banks in the United States, more than one-third fewer than the 14,393 banks that existed in 1985. Banking industry consolidation was also evident in mergers between holding companies, whose numbers declined by 139 last year, to 5,971. The largest fifty holding companies continued to steadily increase their share of industry assets, from 74 percent at the end of 1997 to 76 percent at the end of last year.[1]

Exhibit 2-2 is a sketch of how value is driven by competitive integration M&A. The two primary drivers of competitive integration mergers are revenue increase and operational efficiency. Revenues are increased dramatically through acquisition. This is evident in the exhibit as the revenues for the combined entity are significantly larger than company A and

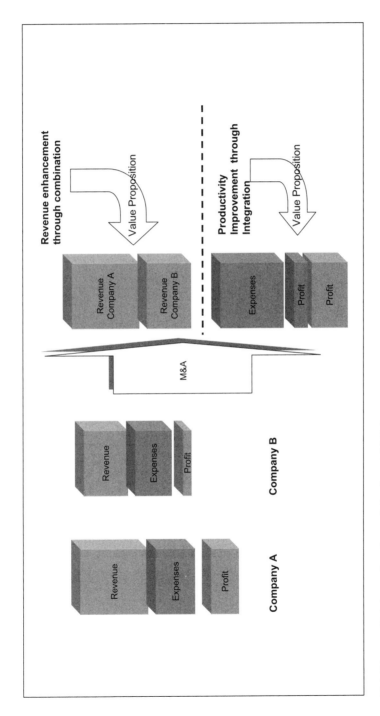

Exhibit 2-2. Driving value through horizontal M&A.

company B. Executives feel that increased market share and geographic presence will enhance the prospect for growth of the combined entity. Operational efficiency results from improved economies of scale. Since both companies are in the same line of business, their operations can be integrated to become more efficient. Unit costs decline, thereby increasing profitability. The dark green bar depicts the profit improvement from economies of scale.

Supply Chain Movement

Supply chain movement M&A is a combination of a company and its buyers or suppliers. General Motors buying an auto parts manufacturer would be an example of a supply chain movement merger. This type of merger allows the acquiring company to reach across the supply chain and take advantage of the benefits available to its trading partners. Supply chain movement mergers and acquisitions typically take one of two forms: 1) supplier acquisitions or 2) buyer acquisitions (see Exhibit 2-3). Shareholder value is derived from supplier acquisitions because these acquisitions eliminate cost layers for materials and services. Shareholder value is derived from buyer acquisitions because these acquisitions enable companies to sell in their markets with lower cost structures and serve the end customer in the supply chain.

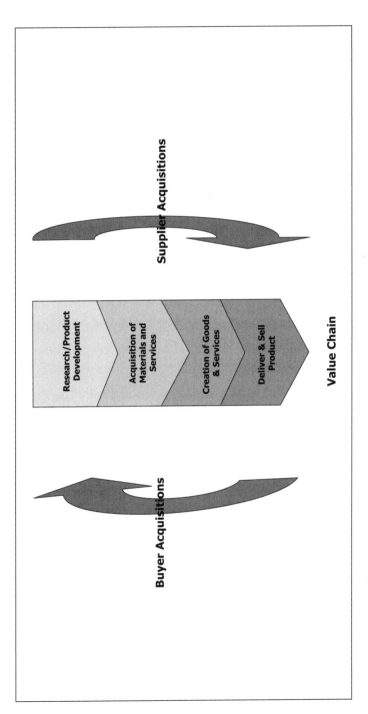

Exhibit 2-3. Supply chain movement.

Supplier Acquisitions

Through supplier acquisitions, margins can be improved by reducing the cost of goods sold. To illustrate, let's look at how a supply chain movement acquisition would improve the cost of production of a hypothetical apparel designer, Ann's Enterprises. The average garment sells for sixty dollars. The total cost per unit is forty dollars. The components of the costs are designated in Exhibit 2-4.

The designer relies on a jobber to produce the clothing at twenty dollars per garment (manufacturing). As illustrated in Exhibit 2-5, the jobber has a cost of production of ten dollars and profit of ten dollars per garment. By purchasing the jobber, unit profits would increase to thirty dollars per garment since the jobber profit has been eliminated. The value proposition is the shift of the jobber profit to the designer as shown by the curved arrow. Value is driven through an improved efficiency as unit profit increases.

Fabric	$ 5
Production	$20
Design	$ 5
General and Administrative	$10
Total	$40

Exhibit 2-4. Design example.

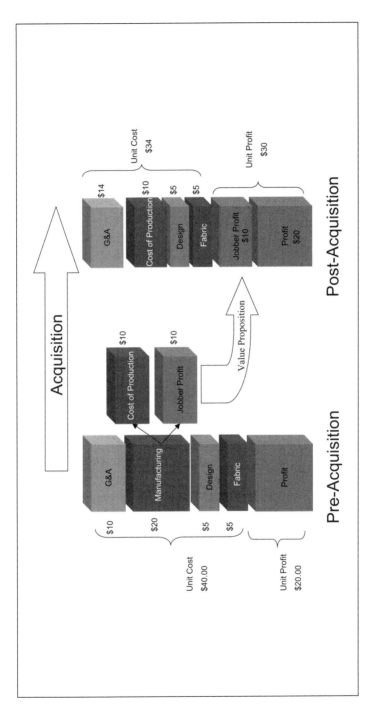

Exhibit 2-5. Supply chain movement and cost reduction.

Buyer Acquisitions

Buyer acquisitions produce a competitive advantage by enabling a company to sell to its customers at a lower price. The advantages are lower cost (similar to supplier acquisitions) and better access to materials. To illustrate, let's look at what would happen if a microchip maker bought a cell phone manufacturer. The buyer would have faster access to new components and improved control over inventory.

Many companies use mergers and acquisitions as a method of outsourcing research and development. From a strategic perspective, supply chain movement acquisition provides companies with a method of acquisition of fresh intellectual capital and new products. This can help reduce competition by capturing new innovation that solidifies market share. Companies may also gain access to substitute products (other product lines not within the current product mix) through acquisition. This strategy is extremely effective in fluid markets such as high tech. The variety of products and speed of change has made it difficult to continually innovate cutting-edge solutions. This type of activity is common in the software industry. Peoplesoft Enterprise Resource Planning software recognized the need to expand its suite of applications to include data presentation capabilities. Peoplesoft's product mix included software solutions for human resources, financial, and e-business applications. Peoplesoft purchased a company called Vantive to extend its product line into data presentation. Product line expansion is also a method of diversification, which we will discuss later in this chapter. It mitigates the risk of having a single product and eliminates pressure from substitute products in the marketplace. It is prevalent in industries that have high levels of product evolution (see Exhibit 2-6).

Diversification

Diversification mergers and acquisitions are combinations of businesses in unrelated industries. One example of this type of business combination is a pickle manufacturer buying a software company. These companies do not compete against each other and are not in the same industry. The strategic issue addressed by diversification combinations is industry risk. The underlying concept behind diversification activity is closely aligned with holding a portfolio of diversified stocks. Investment risk is being spread across numerous industries (see Exhibit 2-7). Lack of performance due to industry conditions in one industry can be offset by superior returns in another. Diversification mergers mitigate the impact of forces emanating from industry pressures by spreading risk across multiple industries or markets. General Electric is a leader in diversification through mergers and acquisitions. It is involved in a diverse set of busi-

(text continues on page 44)

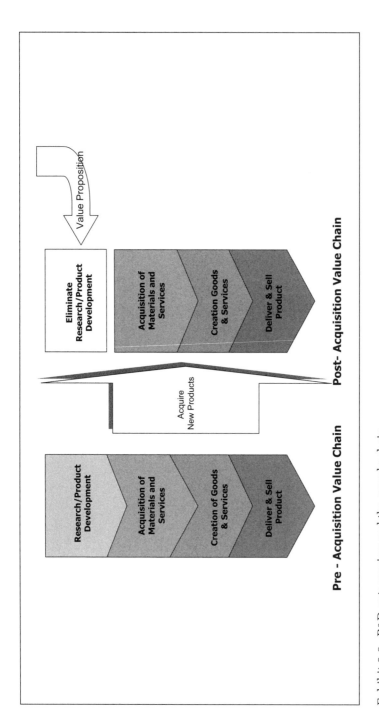

Exhibit 2-6. R&D outsourcing and the supply chain.

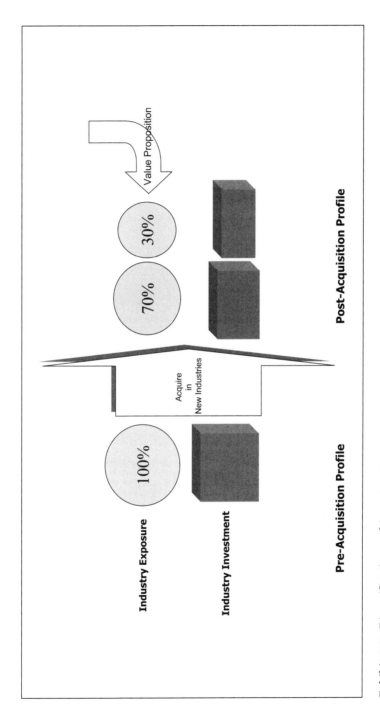

Exhibit 2-7. Diversification and investment.

nesses—from medical equipment to financial services. In the case of the acquisitive pickle manufacturer, its exposure to pressures from suppliers of cucumbers declines because it is less reliant on revenues and profits from pickles. The primary value proposition is driven by revenue increases and a more sustainable cash flow.

Value from diversification combinations may also be derived from efficiency gains. Economies of scale can be attained through integration of business sustaining functions such as finance and human resources. These synergies may not be as great as competitive integration because business-sustaining functions may be specialized within industries. A bank has different reporting requirements than a biotechnology company. The improvement comes from elimination of duplicated functions. A combination of two companies may lead to elimination of administrative staff such as accounting personnel. If both companies have one hundred people in their accounting departments, they may be able to perform the combined accounting function with 120 workers. This results in savings of eighty employees. The elimination of workers, fixed assets, and other duplicated resources leads to an overall reduction of operating expenses in the long run. This assumes that the function performed requires no specialized knowledge of the specific industries.

Risks of Mergers and Acquisitions

There are three distinct risks to mergers and acquisitions: 1) lower interim productivity, 2) completion, and 3) realization of benefits. Each of these risks can be influenced by many factors.

Interim Efficiency Loss

All mergers and acquisitions require operational change that may temporarily compromise short-term financial performance. However, shareholder demand for short-term results in the form of increased earnings from the business combination does not wane. It is critical that the combined business gets to its target margins as soon as possible. This is why the stock of the acquiring company will normally go down after a merger announcement. Effectively managing this risk of efficiency loss is critical to a successful M&A strategy. The impact of these pressures on the ability to integrate effectively underscores the need for accurate forecasting. This is not to say that there will not be variances to budget, but estimates need to be within a gross order of magnitude. Painting an overly optimistic picture of the expected results from mergers and acquisitions can be the worst enemy of the integration team.

M&A Completion

The initial stages of the M&A process are time-con-suming and expensive. In most cases, they involve the most talented individuals in the company. As these individuals are pulled away from their day-to-day responsibilities, business operations may suffer. These efforts are lost if the company cannot identify and successfully close on the appropriate targets. In addition, many transactions are structured with break-up fees if the deal is not consummated.

Realization of Benefits

This issue is at the heart of managing value in a merger. The central question is: When the integration is completed, will the acquirer attain the benefits they envisioned in the strategy and rationale stage of the M&A process? Normally, lower interim productivity is recognized as a risk and accepted by management and shareholders. However, patience wears thin as:

❐ Synergies are not realized. Webster defines synergy as "combined action or operation."[2] Synergies should dramatically improve the competitive position of both firms. Examples of synergies are complementary sales channels, improved market share, supply chain effi-ciencies, and improved product lines. If the synergies are not compelling or attainable, the deal should not be done.

❏ Financial returns are weakened. There is an opportunity for efficiency improvement in all types of mergers (Exhibit 2-8). However, the potential for productivity improvement, and the resulting cost savings, is much greater when the companies have similar processes and technologies.

Combinations that are driven by diversification can target business-sustaining functions such as finance and human resources as potential areas for cost reduction. Competitive mergers have the greatest opportunity in this area because the organizations have similar supply chains. This can improve margins and cut costs per unit. The risk is that fixed costs normally increase to support a larger organization. If revenues soften, then profits will decline and margins weaken. Many mergers are predicated on overly aggressive cuts in expenses that cannot be realized. The causes are unattainable expectations and inability to judge the savings opportunity.

Summary: Mergers and Acquisitions as a Strategic Alternative

Mergers and acquisitions can be rationalized in three ways. Companies merge to achieve competitive inte-

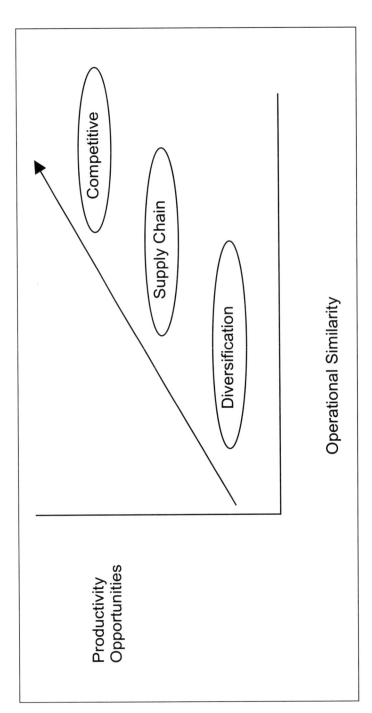

Exhibit 2-8. Financial returns.

gration, supply chain movement, and diversification. Competitive integration is done to increase revenue and take advantage of synergies. Supply chain movements help improve margins, lock up new innovations in the marketplace, and provide access to end customers in the supply chain. Diversification helps companies reduce their exposure to specific industries. The major risks of M&A are the inability to realize economies of scale from synergies, consummation of the transactions themselves, and lower interim productivity that ultimately result in weakened financial performance.

Outsourcing

> *We outsource a number of functions, from help-desk technical support for our employees to the physical production of our software packages. It's far more efficient for many companies, including Microsoft, to have an outside company handle installations and support for desktop machines.*
>
> Bill Gates, *At the Speed of Thought*

Outsourcing is the practice of using third-party resources to perform functions and/or business processes. Virtually any process can be outsourced, from sales to product delivery. Industry experts have sized the global market for outsourcing in the trillions of dollars. The industry continues to grow as businesses recognize the value potential of this strategic alternative.

Types of Outsourcing

The rapid growth of outsourcing indicates a dramatic shift in how we think about our businesses. The management mind-set has changed from control to competence. The key to competitive strategy is now based on management of core competencies and not control over functions. As an example, management used to view having the entire IT function performed by a third party as absurd. Today, many companies outsource the majority of their IT functions. The rise in the cost of implementation and operation of large-scale technology initiatives has fueled tremendous growth in the outsourcing industry. The need for new technology has outstripped the capabilities of many businesses. This has created a gap in both resources and risk. The intensive demand for human capital with knowledge of new technologies has far outstripped the supply of internal resources. Yet at the same time these systems become obsolete very quickly and require major enhancement to stay current with market conditions and business needs.

This trend does not strictly apply to technology. This concept has been extended to business-sustaining functions or business services. Many companies are assessing the viability of outsource arrangements for all general and administrative processes. For example, the finance, payroll, human resource and IT functions are now on the radar screen. Customer service is being outsourced by companies like Microsoft. Many medical insurance providers are contracting out many policy administrative functions as well. Many large firms feel that these functions are no longer a core competency and can be contracted to outside firms. In order to maintain a level of control, they are structuring contracts that involve equity stakes in the outsource provider. The early-stage sales process was never considered an area that could be performed by an outside firm. Now companies have recognized that early-stage sales is an expensive, low-probability process that is best done by a service provider to reduce risk and lower cost.

There are four main reasons for a company to get involved in outsourcing: 1) to increase strategic focus, 2) to improve processes, 3) to reduce costs, and 4) to share risks. In the past many managers have focused solely on cost reduction because it is the easiest to quantify; however, the potential value of the other types of outsourcing is equally compelling.

Strategic Focus

Keeping your sights locked on improvement is an essential part of strategic planning. Identification and execution of core competencies is essential to success. A core competency is a function or process that is critical to the success of a business. Outsourcing allows companies to keep up with best practices in other functions while remaining focused on core competencies. With outsourcing, businesses have access to highly skilled personnel without having to maintain a large staff. This is relevant in information technology. Application service providers (ASPs) develop, maintain, and enhance entire systems, giving clients freedom to focus on their business. This eliminates concerns about hardware/software upgrades, staffing, and training. What is the value proposition? A company's competitive position is improved by focus on what it does best.

Process Improvement

One of the prime reasons for hiring an outsourcing firm is that it can perform processes quicker, more skillfully, and less expensively than you can. Many outsourcing companies are specialists at specific functions. They will do a better job since they are strategically focused on specific tasks. Many companies have chosen to outsource their call center function because outsourcing providers have superior technology and highly trained staff. Since these companies have numerous customers, they can attain the critical mass to twenty-four-hour-a-day service. Customer service can improve because this is the sole focus of the service provider. The value proposition here is an improvement in competitive position through access to best practices and technology.

Cost Reduction

Many companies find it dramatically less expensive to outsource than to perform a function in-house. Companies can show an immediate reduction on operating costs that can be in the double digits. Outsourcing gives businesses the ability to use their partner's economies of scale. Operating expenses are reduced because the function can be performed at lower unit costs through outsourcing versus performing the function with internal resources. Reduced expenses improve margins as shown in Exhibit 2-9, where a company reviewed its value chain, which had costs of $450 million. The company determined that product delivery was not a core competency and decided to outsource this activity. The value proposition is highlighted by the curved arrow on the lower right side of the exhibit. Value is improved by improving profits by $30 million through cost reduction. Strategically, cost structure improvements enhance your competitive position.

Risk Sharing

If a function is outsourced, fixed costs are generally shifted to the service provider. The outsourcing com-

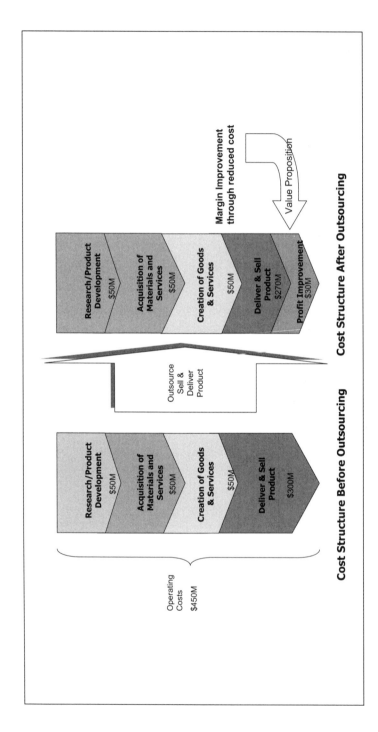

Exhibit 2-9. Driving value through outsourcing.

pany takes on the responsibility of location, equipment, and staff. In the case of a call center, the upfront technology costs alone can be prohibitive. This does not include staffing and maintenance fees and lost productivity from ramp-up of the operation. The outsourcing provider would assume part of the risks of building the operation based on a service contract. Competitive position is improved because the required investment is minimized.

Risks of Outsourcing

Despite the tremendous growth in outsourcing, the failure rate is quite high. "Dun & Bradstreet Barometer of Global found that 25 percent of all firms . . . report an outsourcing relationship failure within the past two years."[3]

Productivity Gaps

A critical thing to remember is that outsourcing is a change in the way you do business. When things change, there is an interim adjustment period that requires significant attention. If this period is not managed correctly, the initiative can fail quickly. With this in mind, the outsourcing contract will specify a learning curve and take over. For example, a company may have outsourced to improve customer service. However, service levels may get worse if the transition process is ill defined. While expense reduction may have been the goal for outsourcing of processes, transition costs would offset initial cost reductions. The risk lies in not containing costs and process burdens within budget and in forecasted time frames.

Process Fit

A business is at risk when outsourced services do not fit tightly into its business model. The looser the fit, the higher the risk. If there are gaps in processes or services, business results may suffer. In an outsourced call center, for example, the customer should not know that they are being served by a third party. The customer experience should be focused on needs and not providers. If the customer's needs are not met, the result may be loss of sales, declines in customer retention, and a loss in competitive position.

Loss of Control

Some companies are reluctant to give up what they believe to be control over some aspect of their business. When a process or piece of the business is performed by a third party, there is less input on how the work is performed. In addition, it may take longer to resolve problems if the function is being performed off-site. Companies that require tight control of the customer experience may find outsourcing too risky for certain functions.

Exit Barriers

Outsourcing leads to limited commitment of internal resources to a process, function, and or infrastructure. The risk is that the business does not have the capacity to perform the function, leaving the firm at the mercy of the service provider. If the outsourcing effort fails, then the company will be forced to find another service provider, or rebuild the competency internally. Fixing the problem then requires unraveling the outsourcing relationship. This, in turn, may cause a disturbance in day-to-day operation of the business. The result will be increased costs from productivity loss and from transitions to new providers or internal capability. Going back to our call center example, it is not simple to turn off the switch on customer service capabilities. Where will the company find the trained staff to service your customers? How would it acquire technology to enable the operation? Can it deploy the business processes to effectively service your customers? What will the impact be to customer retention and sales?

Summary: Outsourcing as a Strategic Alternative

Outsourcing creates value through increasing strategic focus, improving processes, reducing costs, and eliminating risks. Outsourcing gives firms the ability to focus on their core competencies, leaving non-value-added activities to the outsourcing provider. Processes have the potential to be improved because outsourcing providers specialize in performing these services at a lower cost. Risk can be mitigated due to reduced investment levels and elimination of operating expenses. This makes companies more productive in weaker markets as they will have a lower cost structure. The risks of outsourcing include loss of operational control, process fit, loss of productivity, and exit barriers. Outsourcing is truly a partnership. Deriving value from a partnership requires effort from both participants. Businesses that consider outsourcing must be prepared to commit significant time and effort in making the relationship successful.

Conclusion

We examined mergers and acquisitions and outsourcing as external Strategic Alternatives. These are initiatives for which external means have been chosen to accomplish strategic goals. Both of these SAs are extremely common and have high failure rates due to their large impact on financial performance and high-stakes nature. External SAs should be considered as strong methods to execute strategy and increase shareholder value but they need to be assessed carefully. The implications of execution are generally more complex than most executives predict.

Notes

1. Antuilo Bomfirm and William R. Nelson, "Profits and Balance Sheets Developments at U.S. Commercial Banks," *Federal Reserve Bulletin,* Vol. 85, No. 6 (June 1999), pp. 369-395.
2. *Merriam Webster's Collegiate Dictionary,* 10th ed. (1999).
3. Michael F. Corbett & Associates, Ltd., http://www .firmbuilder.com/articles/19/48/388/.

CHAPTER 3

Internal Strategic Alternatives

STRATEGIC ALTERNATIVES are normally viewed as initiatives that are external in nature. Mergers and acquisitions and outsourcing are well publicized and make headlines in major business and industry periodicals. There has been a growing preference toward external Strategic Alternatives that is validated by the growth in the value of mergers as well as the size of outsourcing contracts. Yes, these external means are important and are viable ways to execute against a strategic plan. Yet these alternatives need to be looked at carefully as their effectiveness is not conclusive. On the other hand, internal SAs have taken a backseat in terms of visibility and priority. Internal initiatives, or efforts where internal means are used to develop specific competencies, are equally as important as external SAs, and they are viable ways of increasing value. On balance, internally developed competencies may generate more value in the long run, have lower cultural hurdles to overcome, and have lower switching costs and barriers to exit. It is much harder to unwind a merger or rebuild an outsourced service than to scrap an internal initiative.

This chapter will deal with two of the most common internal SAs—information technology and business process reengineering. (For the purposes of our discussion, the terms IT and technology will be used interchangeably.) Despite the bursting of the Internet bubble in the late 1990s, the strategic use of information technology will continue to grow. We will see a more thoughtful use of technology in the future predicated on economic justification, not marketing hype. This trend has already started with the performance of crude financial tests such as ROI (return on investment) measures. As the size and complexity of IT systems continues to increase, businesses realize that this is something they need to get right—especially since many systems are now shared directly with their customers.

A closely related initiative to IT is business process reengineering (BPR). BPR is a simply a drastic change in what you do as a business. The relationship between these two SAs is that technology projects invariably spawn a reengineering project. Implementations in large-scale technology projects will naturally change the way you conduct business. Of course, BPR can also be implemented as a stand-alone and independent way to increase value. Many large companies have units whose sole function is reengineering of processes. Since drastic change is involved, BPR becomes a high stakes game where the end result can change as fast as the process.

Information Technology

As recently as fifteen years ago, information technology (IT) would have not been viewed as strategic in nature. IT has been elevated to a strategic level for two reasons. First, a company's ability to use technology to improve value is now critical to business success. Technological change impacts all aspects of a business, from backroom operations to customer interaction. Second, technology is becoming a significant part of business investment. Research firms have estimated that business spending on technology has surpassed one trillion dollars. In service-based businesses, IT spending represents a large majority of capital expenditure spending. But what do we mean by IT?

Demystifying Information Technology: What Is IT?

Information technology is considered anything that transports, processes, analyzes, and presents information to a user. In this book we are not necessarily interested in how the technology functions, but whether it can effectively enhance shareholder value and execute corporate strategy. You can think of IT in terms of three building blocks: infrastructure, data, and software (Exhibit 3-1). The technological infrastructure is the foundation upon which the technological pyramid is built. Like any building, without a strong foundation the structure will fall down. The infrastructure needs to support the weight of the data and software components of the pyramid. If your PC crashes because it does not have adequate memory to support the software application that you want to run, then the technical infrastructure of your computer is inadequate.

The infrastructure is made up of items like PC servers, mainframes, T-1 lines (an optical fiber phone line), and routers. The cost of the infrastructure is normally a small part of the total pyramid. When infrastructure investments are made in isolation, they are difficult to evaluate because the benefits are normally derived from the data and software layers. These types of investments also have the risk of being evaluated as sunk costs, or costs that should not be associated with other technology investments.

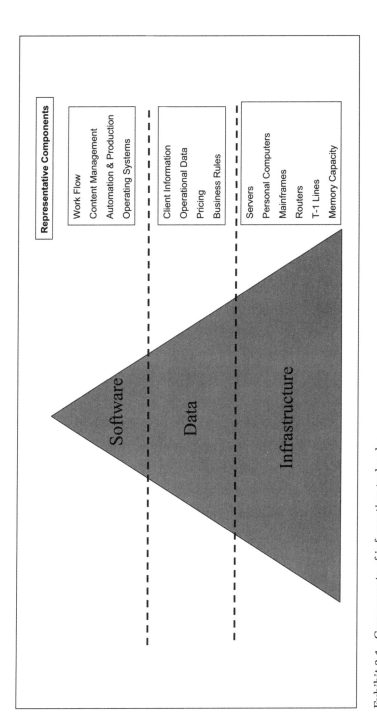

Exhibit 3-1. Components of information technology.

The data block of the pyramid is extremely valuable. It holds all the information about your company and customers. (The value of many companies is based solely on their customer base.) The data block also is the repository for your intellectual capital. This can include business rules, which are an automated version of your processes. The software block is responsible for leveraging the data and infrastructure to use information effectively. Types of software continue to proliferate. Systems are moving from automation of internal processes such as financial systems that perform accounting functions to external processes that link buyers and suppliers together. Software systems have become mission-critical to many businesses. If systems are not running, many businesses cannot operate. IT is now the backbone of the securities business, where trades are executed electronically and manual processes have become the exception, as opposed to business as usual.

Rationale for Information Technology

Many companies have a great deal of difficulty validating the value derived from technology because the benefits of technology are not easily translated into financial terms. The increase in revenues from combining companies is much more visible than the impact of implementing sales force automation software. One of the clearly linked benefits of information technology is revenue enhancement.

Revenue Enhancement

As a company's technology is made available to customers, the use of technology can be directly linked to creating revenue. The purest example of revenue enhancement through the use of technology is e-commerce. Retail sales over the Internet are the fastest-growing retail channel. As consumers have grown accustomed to the conveniences of shopping online, Internet sales have grown dramatically. Another technology application that increases sales is the use of kiosks, where no human intervention is necessary to sell a product. This technology is being used to purchase anything from subway fares to airline tickets.

Competitive Intelligence

IT helps create competitive intelligence through the use of information about internal business processes and customer information. CRM (customer relations management) systems provide a competitive advantage by collecting information about customer behaviors. Retailers use these systems to connect its order information with customer profiles. This gives retailers an advantage over their competition because they get insights into purchasing patterns by customer, demographic profile, and geographic information.

Let's assume that a national furniture retailer discovers through its sales information system that brown leather couches are a hot seller on the East Coast. Armed with this information, the retailer can feature brown couches on its catalog covers and website in that specific geographic market. The retailer will sell more of these couches than competitors who do not have the benefits of this intelligence.

Another way of increasing sales of this product is to create call center processes that pitch brown couches when a customer inputs an East Coast zip code. The retailer can also improve its operations by stocking more brown couches for its East Coast Stores; this increases cash flow by getting the fast-selling products to the stores and keeping the slow-selling furniture off the store floor.

Let's look at an example of competitive intelligence on the other end of the supply chain. How can a company use information to cut its costs of purchasing goods and materials? IT systems can be used to collect buying information that helps firms negotiate better discounts with suppliers. Many large companies that operate numerous locations are often not able to track purchasing on a company-wide basis. E-procurement systems can connect the purchasing activity in the various sites and pool the consumption patterns. Assume that National Corp. operates ten locations throughout the West Coast. Each location annually spends $200,000 with different vendors for office supplies. Among these vendors is Super Supplier with stores across the country—they presently service one location with revenue from National of $200,000. An e-procurement system can help National understand what is being purchased and by whom. Using e-procurement, National finds that it spends a total of $2,000,000 in office supplies—mostly on commodity items that are not location specific. National can take that information and negotiate volume discounts with an office supply company to provide services to the buyer on a national basis. As a result of having this information, the company can cut its costs on office supplies, National is able to negotiate a 10 percent discount on its purchase—saving the company $200,000. Super Supplier, the successful bidder for the National contract, benefits by increasing its sales from $200,000 to $1,800,000.

Efficiency Improvements

IT can improve cash flow through process automation. Many manual components of processes can be performed through automation that is faster and cheaper than the manual alternative. Many ERP software packages issue checks without any human intervention.

One example of using technology to improve efficiency is the company 1-800-FLOWERS. The strategic use of IT helped transform the company into a multimillion-dollar telephone and Web-based florist with a global reach. The company used to rely heavily on advertising because it could not retain its customers. It had a cumbersome manual order-taking process. Telephone representatives needed to write the order, get credit card approval, find the closest participating florist to the delivery location, choose the floral arrangement, and send the order to the florist. When the company automated the order-taking process, sales started to grow at a higher rate as a result of the improved service. The efficiency of the order-taking staff improved since the manual aspects of the process were eliminated. Consequently, labor costs were limited.

How does IT help reduce costs? One way information technology can cut labor costs is through staff reduction. Let's look at a concrete example of this: Ford Motor Company's implementation of an invoice-free processing system that resulted in large reductions in labor costs. Ford needed more than 500 people in its North American accounts payable (A/P) department. A/P staff spent most of their time trying to resolve discrepancies between purchase orders, receiving documents, and invoices. Ford implemented an IT system that used the Web to have vendors enter purchase orders into an online database. Then the purchase orders were verified by the receiving department upon shipment arrival. If the shipment matched the purchase order, the system generated a check to the vendor. This processing system eliminated the need for vendors to send invoices. The technology reduced the head count in accounts payable significantly and improved the accuracy of financial information.

E-procurement systems can cut purchasing costs for goods and services as well by significantly reducing the amount of research required to find the best price for a product. The search engine within the e-procurement system can locate the top supplier for a specific product in a manner of seconds. This eliminates time-consuming searches for product suppliers. These systems also collect buying information that can be used to negotiate better discounts with suppliers. Often large companies that operate numerous locations are not able to track purchasing on a company-wide basis. E-procurement systems connect the purchasing activity in the various sites and pool the consumption patterns. The companies using the systems gain leverage over their suppliers since they can make the case for steeper discounts.

Information technology and business process reengineering (bpr) are close cousins. Most technology initiatives involve changes to the way work is done in a business. Things as simple as using e-mail can mean a drastic change in the way employees communicate internally and externally. The implications are significant. When technology is implemented there will be:

❏ A change in the way employees do their jobs

❏ A period where people will need to learn the technology

❏ A negative impact to productivity

These factors are often ignored in the planning phase of a technological initiative. In many cases these questions have been avoided because the technology was used internally. As a company's technology is pushed out to customers (such as in the self-service example above), the impact can become much greater. This means that many of the risks of BPR initiatives that we will discuss later in this chapter can also be attributed to IT projects.

Risks of IT

There are several risks in implementing IT projects.

Channel Cannibalization

To understand the risk of channel cannibalization we have to go back to our retailer who is selling brown leather couches. What if existing customers decided to buy through the Internet instead of through the stores? The customer may not purchase any more merchandize on-site from the retailer, but will move his purchases to the Internet. Why is this a risk? Any e-commerce initiative may decrease cash flow in the short run because you are supporting two channels to make the same amount of revenue. For example, people may *shop* on the Internet but *buy* the products on-site in the stores. You may not be able to cut back on store costs to compensate for lowered sales volume on the channel.

Adoption Rate

Value can only be generated from an IT initiative if it is used. If our hypothetical company National cannot get its employees to buy office supplies on the e-procurement system, then it will not cut its purchasing costs by implementing this technology. Adoption rate is a measure of utilization of a system. It is expressed as the percentage of the total user base that adopts or leverages the use of the technology. The adoption rate needs to be analyzed for risk purposes. The assumption of a 100 percent adoption rate is unrealistic. Many business cases have been built on the inaccurate assumption that full adoption of the system will occur upon installation. For example, benefit projections for e-procurement could assume that all spending occurs through the system the day that it is put into service.

Let's look at a large financial institution that had installed a loan approval system. The system gave employees the ability to analyze loan requests without using any paper. The system would then update and notify other divisions about loan decisions, eliminating the need for phone calls, faxes, and e-mails. With benefits like these, you would think that everyone would like to use the system. Unfortunately, the underwriters, or decision makers on these loans, refused to use the system. The underwriters complained that the system was more difficult to use than old-fashioned pen and paper. They said they had to wade through eight different screens to render an approval on a loan. It actually took longer to approve a loan with the technology than it did manually. The system was simply used as a tracking device. Communication was done the old way. Since the underwriters did not use the system, cash flow declined due to increased technology costs with no benefits stream.

Experience with Technology

Risk increases if a firm lacks experience with a specific technology. If business is not familiar with specific hardware, software, or operating systems, it is likely that the SA will experience timing delays and cost overruns and fail to deliver the expected benefits. Companies also lose management control of the implementation as they are at the mercy of outside contractors. Control is even more difficult when the users of the technology are less likely to be corporate employees. This extends the concept of technological experience beyond your organizations to buyers and suppliers. A potential risk of the system implemented by Ford could have been the technological readiness of the vendors to use the Web-based system. In many cases, vendors with leverage over their customers will not adopt these systems because they may see them as a threat.

Obsolescence

Many would say that the risk of technological obsolescence is overhyped. Systems and hardware function for years well beyond their intended life span. The risk of obsolescence is related to a system's ability to integrate with other systems. As systems age, their ability to support interfaces with newer technology greatly diminishes. It becomes more timely and expensive to connect systems together and retrieve information from them.

Summary: Information Technology as a Strategic Alternative

IT is emerging as a critical means of putting strategy into action. IT distributes processes and analyzes information. Information technology can be divided into three components: software, data, and infrastructure. Infrastructure supports the technology architecture and consists of hardware, memory, and communications equipment. Data is the actual information that includes everything from client contact information to the procedures by which a business is run. Software links the infrastructure and the data together to use information. IT can improve cash flow and consequently value through enhancing revenue (making Internet sales), gaining competitive intelligence (capturing customer information), and improving operational efficiency (automating manual processes). The risks of IT include lack of adoption, inexperience with technology, and obsolescence. The majority of IT initiatives have an impact on how work is done and require changes to business processes. Hence, IT projects also have the same risks as business process reengineering, which we will discuss next.

Business Process Reengineering

Business process reengineering (BPR) involves radically changing a process in order to increase efficiency. The term was first coined by Michael Hammer and James Champy in their book *Reengineering the Corporation: A Manifesto for Business Revolution.* The radical difference between business process reengineering and the traditional view of running a business is the focus on the process of how a company operates as opposed to focusing on specific functions such as production, marketing, engineering, finance, and human resources. Companies are generally organized around functional lines. This functional alignment creates silos that tend to slow the work flow and create inefficiencies. The BPR perspective is that companies are divided into core processes, such as strategy creation, product innovation, sales, manufacturing, and customer service. These processes tend to cut across numerous functions. BPR specialists contend that the optimal mode of operation is to run a company based on processes and not on function. This improves the efficiency and the competitive position of the firm through higher profits, faster time to market, and ability to respond to customers.

Managers make changes to the way business is done on a day-to-day basis. If these efforts occur regularly, why would we consider BPR a strategic alternative as opposed to ongoing operations? BPR tends to have major implications on a company's competitive ability as well as on its financial performance. Since BPR affects both strategy and finance, it is critical to evaluate BPR by linking these implications together and validating that the strategic use of BPR results in improvements in intrinsic value. In this book, our discussion will address large-scale efforts that would likely produce swings in value.

BPR initiatives usually have the following characteristics that would portend large strategic implications and intrinsic value:

❒ Top-down-driven initiative

❒ Dramatic shifts in day-to-day operations

❒ Enterprise use of technology to create efficiencies.

Since IT and BPR initiatives are interrelated, how can you make the distinction between the two Strategic Alternatives? The difference lies in what is driving the benefits of the SA. If the objective is solely to change an existing business process, then the initiative is a reengineering. Many technology initiatives do not involve large-scale changes in work processes and there are reengineering initiatives that do not have major technology components.

Top-Down-Driven Initiative

BPR efforts that originate from the higher levels of a business will tend to have greater repercussions than those that begin in the middle management ranks. These efforts are not simple modifications to business processes occurring in the normal course of business and tend to change the entire business model of a company. Hence, a BPR initiative that is considered a

SA is a stand-alone project involving the sponsorship of senior management. Let's look at a sports example to illustrate this distinction. If the coaching staff of a football team changes the play book, this would be a strategic reengineering. A quarterback making a change to a running play based on the pursuit of the defense is a modification to the business process in the normal course of a game. The coaches can be compared to executives in a top-down BPR.

Dramatic Operational Shifts

When a process is redesigned there is a radical difference in how things get done. The following diagram illustrates the magnitude of the change between the current and target (reengineered) process in a loan-granting function. The current process includes three reviews of a loan application by different employees: the salesperson, the manager, and the analyst before an approval can be made (Exhibit 3-2).

The target process dramatically changes the work flow by eliminating the initial review by the salesperson and the manager. A loan application can potentially be approved without human intervention. The benefits of the new process are tremendous (the financial benefits of this example will be discussed later). The target process frees up time of the analyst, manager, and salesperson creating organizational efficiency. The organization has a much greater capac-

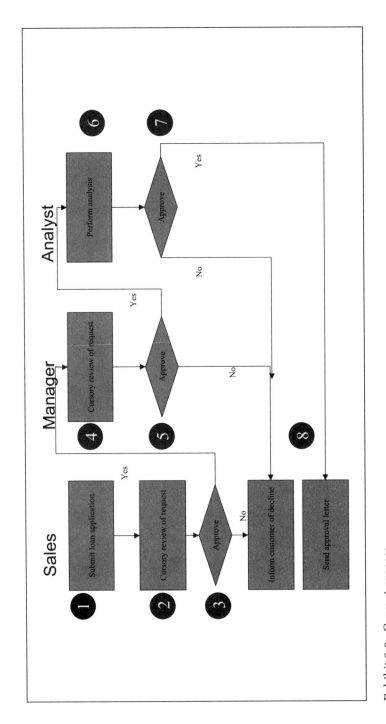

Exhibit 3-2. Current process.

ity to process loan applications because the number of reviews is reduced, meaning applicants experience a faster decision time. Exhibit 3-3 shows the makeup of this change.

Enterprise Use of Technology to Create Efficiencies

One of the key drivers in reengineering efforts is the use of technology to create efficiencies in the improved process. This is also the "Achilles heel" of reengineering projects. The success of the entire effort hinges on whether the technological solution is fully utilized. The important thing to remember is that the technology will be used across your entire business. The technology will do one of two things:

1. It will perform a particular function, as shown in our loan-granting example, where the initial screening of a loan is performed by the system as opposed to a salesperson.

2. The technology will probably become the glue that binds work functions together. Going back to our loan example, the system is routing loans back to sales after they are approved.

Work flows are designed, metrics established, and staffing levels achieved with the assumption that

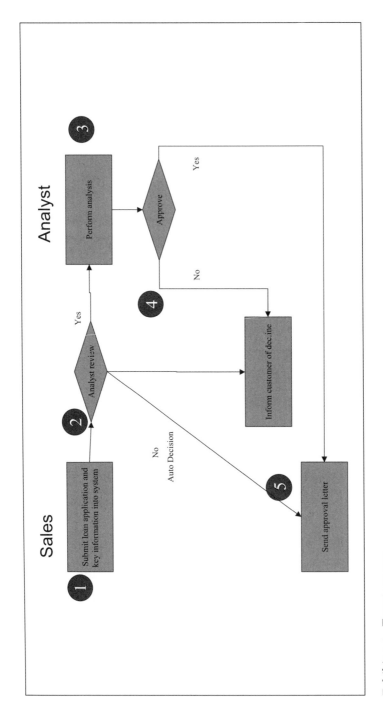

Exhibit 3-3. Target process.

workers will be capitalizing on the use of a system. In many of these efforts technology is the linchpin in the BPR initiative.

Rationale for BPR

The justification for BPR is normally found in two areas: efficiency and competitive repositioning. Since these efforts involve a large amount of change, it seems that many BPRs tend to have their value proposition change along with the effort. This is a slippery slope, which may result in not accomplishing anything. The executive team should have an extremely high degree of clarity around the objective for this effort, especially when the goal is competitive repositioning.

Efficiency

A major benefit of reengineering is that it drives down costs. Most reengineering business cases are extremely compelling. The improvement in margins and profitability can be dramatic. To illustrate the extent of cost reduction, let us compare the cost of approving a loan in the current process and the reengineered process presented earlier. Labor costs are driven down in two ways—through time reduction and step elimination. Time reduction is a simple concept. Time is money. Assume that the analyst in the loan-granting process reduces the time he needs to review a loan from two hours to thirty minutes by using technology. If his hourly labor rate is fifteen dollars, then his labor cost per loan is thirty dollars using the current process. In the reengineered environment, the cost would be $7.50. The total labor cost in the reengineered process is 75 percent lower than in the current process. Second, the reengineered environment mitigates the number of steps required to perform a process. Looking at the financial implications of the process changes illustrated in Exhibits 3-2 and 3-3, the current environment requires eight steps to render a loan decision. At most it takes five steps to make a decision in the reengineered process. The elimination of these steps results in savings of approximately twenty-six dollars per loan. The cost per loan declines by 55 percent if an analyst reviews the loan and 90 percent if it is automatically approved (see Exhibit 3-4).

Market Share Enhancement Through Cycle Time Reduction

Cycle time is the time it takes to perform a certain process. We talked about how time increases efficiency. Reducing process time helps the competitive position of a business. Competitive abilities improve by reducing the time it takes to accomplish a project, process, or a reaction to customers. The definition of

Table Cost Reduction Illustration—Loan Granting

		Current		
Step	Employee	Time (minutes)	Labor Cost (per hour)	Cost of step
1	Sales	15	20	$5.00
2	Sales	10	20	$3.33
3	Sales	5	20	$1.67
4	Manager	10	25	$4.17
5	Manager	5	25	$2.08
6	Analyst	90	15	$22.50
7	Analyst	10	15	$2.50
8	Sales	20	20	$6.67
Total		165		$47.92

		Reengineered (Analyst Review)		
Step	Employee	Time (minutes)	Labor Cost (per hour)	Cost of step
1	Sales	15	20	$5.00
2	NA	1		$0.00
3	Analyst	30	15	$7.50
4	Analyst	10	15	$2.50
5	Sales	20	20	$6.67
Total		76		$21.67

		Reengineered (System Review)
Step	Employee	Time (minutes)
1	Sales	15
2	NA	1
3	NA	0
4	NA	0
5	Sales	20
		36

Exhibit 3-4. Cost reduction.

project completion is broad in scope—it could mean anything from product development to rolling out new technology. Process completion is critical in a fast-moving environment. Compression of the product development process is critical in high technology.

The product life cycle is so sensitive to cycle time that delays narrow the window of competitive advantage for a business. Let's take the microchip business as an example. If a chip is delayed by a month, it may result in the erosion of a company's competitive advantage. This creates a pool of cash, or market demand, waiting to be taken by a competitor. The first entrant into the marketplace can capture a higher share (market share) of this demand before its competitors.

The first entrant into the marketplace also enjoys the ability to charge a higher price. Prices of chips decline rapidly over time, making it more difficult to recover research and development investments and compress profits because unit costs remain the same.

Efficient Resource Consumption

Firms can optimize the use of resources by reengineering. Resources are anything that costs money, such as people, materials, and computer time. The loan-granting process can be improved through shifting resources in steps four and five from high-cost management time to lower-cost analytical staff (see again Exhibit 3-4). Management review time is no longer required, saving approximately six dollars per loan. In the reengineered process, the responsibility of sales is to enter the application into the digital approval system. This creates a win situation for sales staff. The elimination of steps two and three allows salespeople to sell more by focusing their efforts on calling potential applicants, which increases their income potential. They no longer need to be involved in screening loan applications. The bank benefits lower its costs per loan.

Risks of Reengineering

We mentioned earlier that the business cases for reengineering are extremely compelling. Any bank CEO would want to dramatically reduce her cost per loan. Yet, why do BPR efforts fail? There are four major risk points in a reengineering engagement:

1. Unreasonable expectations
2. Lack of sustained executive commitment
3. Resistance to change
4. Technology performance failures

Unreasonable Expectations

We mentioned that a distinctive feature of BPR is that it involves large-scale change. Politically speaking, big changes require large incremental benefits to be accepted. Many of these efforts are justified by astronomical cost savings. This creates a vicious cycle of exaggeration and overcommitment to unattainable goals. The proponents of these types of initiatives will tend to hype the benefits of BPR just to get approval to move forward. The decision makers will demand more, and the proponents of the effort will overpromise just to get the initiative approved. This puts the SA at risk by overlaying unreasonable expectations on an effort that would deliver strong benefits. This feeds the next risk.

Lack of Sustained Executive Commitment

BPR efforts are difficult to execute and often encounter delays in progress. This tends to test the resolve of the executives who have sponsored the SA. As delays occur resulting from resistance to change, short-term operational disruption, and technology, senior management will look to terminate the effort, since the operation has gotten worse as opposed to better. The loan origination capability of the bank described above could have gone from two days for an approval to three days because the staff is getting used to the new process. This would cause customer complaints, declines in customer satisfaction, and loss of revenue to the bank. Since executives have been sold on improvements in customer service and cycle times, they would begin to question the effort. If things do not improve, then they may want to scrap the effort entirely. These types of disruptions also exert political pressure on the executive sponsors. Being associated with a large-scale failure could be a career-ending occurrence. Executives do not want to be associated with a failure and will tend to distance themselves from the initiative. The bar of success may have been set unrealistically high to push the initiative forward. The frustration caused by delays and political exposure may be enough to scuttle the effort, leaving angry employees, customers, and a great deal of money spent with no benefit stream.

Resistance to Change

All humans are creatures of habit, and change is not welcome unless it is absolutely necessary. Doing things differently is uncomfortable and inconvenient for most employees. Just because a new process makes logical sense does not mean that people will embrace change. For example, there was going to be a change in the renewals process for commercial lines of credit for a regional bank. The existing process was causing customer service problems for the bank's existing customers. Customers had been complaining that the process took too long, required too much information, and rehashed details that the bank already covered. The bank was losing accounts to competitor banks in the region that touted hassle-free renewals. The effort to change the renewals process was sponsored by both the president and the CEO of the bank. This was considered a reengineering effort because it affected the largest customers of the bank and cut across two major functions of the operation. The team that was created to spearhead this effort worked with the bank officers and staff to construct a process that would eliminate unnecessary work steps and diminish the functional barriers. The team was careful not to expose the bank to inordinate risk by changing its processes. In a series of meetings, all those involved agreed to the new processes and procedures, and no one voiced a dissenting opinion about the new way of doing things. The president of the bank made sure that the procedures were put in place quickly.

After one month everyone was still doing things the old way. It was discovered that the chief risk officer (although he had verbally endorsed the process) was resisting the change. He stated that he would not approve any renewals using the new process. This is one example of how resistance to change can come at any level of the organization and can foil any BPR.

Technology Performance Failures

Many reengineering efforts do not increase value because the technology that was expected to be the linchpin in the effort does not work. This can happen for many of the reasons stated above. Since employees are depending on technology to help them perform daily functions, weak performance of technology will render the new processes dysfunctional. This risk can also cause resistance to change, as well as loss of executive sponsorship. For instance, ERP systems were supposed to deliver seamless integration of functions. These implementations were notorious for dismantling a perfectly good process and replacing it with laborious, time-consuming processes that required more work than the original way of doing things.

Summary: Reengineering as a Strategic Alternative

By now you should have a clear picture of reengineering. This Strategic Alternative has many compelling positive and negative features. There are various instances where reengineering is a viable solution to creating shareholder value. This SA should be considered when you feel that the way your business is operating can be improved by breaking down functional barriers and removing needless tasks in business processes. The benefits of reengineered processes are increased efficiency, market share enhancement, and better resource consumption. The risks are unreasonable expectations, lack of sustained executive commitment, resistance to change, and technology performance failure.

Conclusion

Information technology and business process reengineering are internal means by which you can execute on
strategy and improve value. The scope of these initiatives is large-scale in nature when they have dramatic
impacts to the operation of your company. IT and BPR
have become interrelated because IT projects involve
changes in the way business is conducted and BPR
often depends on technology systems to provide critical
links in business processes. The relationship between
these SAs leads to a sharing of benefits and risk.

PART 2

The Macro View

CHAPTER 4

The Economic Filter

BUILDING A BRIDGE between strategy and finance requires an analysis of economic factors that affect a business. A macroview of market conditions provides the first level of validation of Strategic Alternatives. This chapter will discuss the economic filter in the Step-Wise Approach to Value (Exhibit 1-1). This filter tests whether Strategic Alternatives (SAs) create shareholder value based on future economic conditions. How do economic factors affect shareholder value? Economic factors impact shareholder value through their influence on market demand (MD). MD measures the total revenue stream for an industry.

We will examine the concept of MD, the economic factors that affect it, and how to vet a Strategic Alternative based on the future direction of MD. The economic factors that we will discuss are GNP, inflation, interest rates, and resource availability. Evaluation of Strategic Alternatives then involves analysis of two factors—MD alignment and equivalence of response. The alignment factor looks at how well the SA accommodates the expansion or contraction in MD. Equivalence of response vets an SA in terms of permanency of market change and market risk. On the basis of these factors, you can determine whether to dismiss the SA or move on to the next filter.

What Is Market Demand and Why Is It Important?

Estimating the growth rate for your business is an important part of your strategic plan. Pricing, product, and channel decisions are vastly different between high growth and mature industries. Investment decisions will require different assumptions and risk profiles as well as the level of resources required to execute an effective strategy. The growth in the technology marketplace is vastly different from the demand for cereal or other mature markets. As these technology markets mature, expansion will slow.

Market demand represents the total revenue

stream for a particular product or service. As mentioned, market demand is simply calculated as follows:

Product Price × **Number of Buyers** = **Market Demand.**

Market demand is a measure of the overall revenue generated by an industry. The value proposition of a Strategic Alternative must include ways to increase value-based shifts in market demand. If market demand is increasing, the value proposition of a Strategic Alternative must be able to capture the increase in potential revenue in the marketplace. If the market is contracting, the value propositions must protect existing demand and focus on efficiency. Alignment with the market requires careful thought. The importance of using this screen can be demonstrated through a consulting experience.

A number of years ago, a client asked for the results of a consulting study to be presented to the board of directors. The consulting team had created an operating unit to support lending to small businesses for a regional bank. Most of their customers were small businesses, and they wanted to apply small business-lending practices to their existing portfolio to increase efficiency as well as to attract new customers by processing loans faster. The value proposition for creating the unit was based on productivity, more specifically improving the bank's cost position. The bank was interested in improving their cost to process a loan and in reducing customer response time. In preparing for the presentation, the focus was on cost reduction and process reengineering. Prior to the board meeting, a separate meeting was conducted with the president and chief operating officer of the bank about the members of the board and their areas of interest. The board consisted of major shareholders and regional business leaders.

As consultants normally do, I worked throughout the night distilling months of work into a concise and focused presentation. The value proposition was clear, quantifiable, and aligned with my client's goals. I arrived at the bank's headquarters confident and excited about the work that had been done. I've always found the most gratifying aspect of my work to be the final presentation. It demonstrates the value of the work. I was the second presenter on the agenda and was instructed to sit at the front of the room next to a tall and thin man in his late fifties. Not having had the pleasure of knowing him, I introduced myself. He was an investor in the bank and asked me what I was presenting. After explaining the purpose of the engagement, he quickly shot back a question to me: "What is the market for the product? If there is no market for this product, then it does not make sense to go forward." This question took me by surprise after spending a month looking at productivity. Fortunately, I was able to respond with a U.S. market demand figure, a growth rate, and an industry profit margin relative to other products.

What can we learn from this experience? Whatever the value proposition, it should be validated with market demand. The value proposition needs to be aligned with the direction of the market demand. The logic behind the key issue in the investor's line of questioning was, "Why do something if there is no demand to support it?" What is unique about this story is that most executives would not associate productivity with market demand. Yet even in this case the line of inquiry was appropriate. Applying an economic filter to all value propositions is important to evaluate strategic alternatives of all types.

Economic Factors that Drive Market Demand

By linking the business planning process to the economic environment, business managers are better equipped to understand whether Strategic Alternatives are creating value. Assessment of the economy involves both examining current conditions and analyzing the future economic outlook based on selected current economic factors. To make more meaningful and complete assumptions, businesses sometimes build forecasting models. Such models can provide a more realistic understanding of possible outcomes and the risks inherent in your business. In order to build a forecasting model, it is important to create and validate a framework for economic (and financial) forecasting. This can involve one or more of the following:

❏ Identifying data patterns and applying time series modeling techniques

❏ Modeling and forecasting your key business drivers

❏ Selecting and using appropriate measures in your forecasting model

❏ Simulating a complete forecast

❏ Dealing with uncertainty

❏ Weighing approaches to interest rate risk modeling

The importance of these specific economic factors in your business is validated through statistical techniques such as regression analysis (discussed in Chapter 9). Here are some prevalent indicators used in analyzing the economy:

❏ Gross national product (GNP)

❏ Gross domestic product (GDP)

❏ Inflation (deflation) CPI

❏ Interest rates

Gross National Product

"GNP measures the output of the citizens of the U.S. and the income from assets owned by U.S. entities, regardless of where they are located."[1]

Since GNP includes output from multinational corporations, it may not be a true indication of how the U.S. economy is performing. This has led to the development of GDP, gross domestic product, a refined picture of the economy that is limited to domestic production.

GNP in mature economies such as the United States grows at a much slower rate than in emerging nations. The growth of output is measured in real terms, meaning that increases in output due to inflation have been removed.

Gross Domestic Product

GDP is defined as "the total value of goods and services produced within the borders of the United States, regardless of who owns the assets or the nationality of the labor used in producing that output."[2] The growth of output is measured in real terms, meaning increases in output due to inflation have been removed.

GDP growth is used to forecast demand for goods and services. Since GDP is an indicator of the economy as a whole, it may not reflect production within various segments of the economy. The U.S. economy continues to mature and growth rates will moderate. The present Federal Reserve policy attempts to hold economic growth to an annual rate of 3 percent.

Inflation (Deflation) CPI

Inflation and deflation are two of the key drivers of product-pricing decisions. Inflation, or increased costs of goods and services, tends to erode profits and exert upward pressure on prices to customers. Price increases to your customers without increases in your costs improve profits. Inflation needs to be analyzed in the context of your firm's buyers, suppliers, and timing of price increases. Inflation can be economically destructive because it creates an upward spiral in prices.

Deflation is a downward force in prices. Deflationary pressures also require careful consideration to determine their effect on your business. Downward pricing pressures may also have negative effects on businesses and the economy as a whole as they decrease GDP. Global pricing pressures force U.S. firms to reduce prices, thus lowering profits. Lower prices require increased unit sales to attain the same revenue.

Interest Rates

Interest rates are a closely watched economic indicator. They are driven by inflation and have a significant impact on economic sectors that require use of debt for asset acquisition such as real estate, heavy equipment, and financial services. Relatively low interest rates portend increased economic activity as the cost of acquisition declines. Low interest rates fuel home buying because the costs of owning a home (monthly mortgage payments) decrease. Cost advantages from lower rates are temporary as product prices increase to reflect elevated demand. Low rates will bring more potential buyers to the residential real estate market bidding up prices of homes and eventually erasing the cost advantage of low interest rates. Conversely, demand for products may decline as interest rates increase.

Interest rates are an important component of planning because they are an indicator of economic growth and can change the viability of long-term investments.

Resource Availability: Land, Labor, Capital, and Technology

What does your business need to implement your strategy? What is the resource availability and cost? Where can you get them? The nature of how we do business is shifting continually. Managers are continuously identifying less expensive and more productive resources. The shift is from domestic tightly controlled resource pools to global, virtual, and option-oriented environments. Manufacturers locate themselves in cheaper markets to minimize production costs and environmental restraints. For example, companies are opening software development facilities in Ireland and India due to the availability of skilled labor at a lower cost.

The flow of capital continues to become more global. Investment in foreign markets is growing, and global investors are increasing their holdings in the U.S. As capital flows are facilitated, firms are pressured to deliver results because investors can easily move into other investments.

As the demand for technology increases, the investment required to obtain state-of-the-art technology is becoming prohibitive. Many businesses have reduced technology costs through outsourcing (contracting with a third-party service provider). Businesses have restrained the growth of production costs through reengineering and increased use of technology. This is a critical element of success. Intensified competition in mature markets has left little room for price increases to improve profits.

Resource availability changes with market demand. Demand for resources increases as markets grow, which puts more pressure on managers to acquire and retain resources. Many managers view resource management as a cost containment issue. This view is shortsighted because it does not focus on increasing value, but on reducing cost. The reality is that continued cost reduction without top line (revenue improvement) is a strategy that will put a firm out of business.

Validation of Strategic Alternatives Using the Economic Screen Alignment with Market Demand

Finding opportunities in a state of continual economic evolution requires vigilance of emerging trends and structural changes in markets. Managers need to understand the competitive forces at work that will shape the future and the linkages to market position. Validation of new ideas requires a deeper understanding of the financial implications of strategy in the short and long run. These insights are gleaned from intrinsic value analysis (Chapter 11).

If Strategic Alternatives are not aligned with market demand, the result can be the destruction of value. Efficiency-driven alternatives such as reengineering can destroy value if the end result is an organization that cannot accommodate new demand. Many reengineering efforts are shortsighted and do not take into account increases in future demand. Assume an order entry operation is reengineered and the capacity of the operation is cut from 10,000 orders per day to 8,000 orders per day, the profit per unit is $2,000, and the implementation time frame is six months. If demand goes back up in six months to 10,000 orders, then the orders opportunity cost would be:

- ❐ The inability to process 2,000 orders
- ❐ The cost to restaff the operation
- ❐ The cost of implementation of the reengineering

On the other hand, if market demand is declining, it may be irrational to introduce innovative new business models, as the market will not support them.

Equivalence of Response

Balancing long- and short-term feedback is the key to success. Delivering immediate financial results must not come at the expense of the future viability of the business. This means that Strategic Alternatives must respond to market changes in a manner that is consistent with the nature of the changes. How do you measure the potential impact of market changes? Two factors can be used to understand impact—permanency and risk.

Permanency

Permanency of the change can be judged along a continuum. The extremes of the continuum are structural and aberrant (Exhibit 4-1). Structural changes reflect permanent changes in the marketplace. These changes may cause a company to reshape its strategy. An illustration of a structural change is the globalization of the U.S. economy. Globalization of markets has forced companies to rethink their business models. Companies have changed the way they do business to accommodate customers from different countries.

Aberrant changes are short-lived in nature. Short-term spikes in interest rates are examples of aberrant changes. Short-term changes can be accommodated by modifications in the resource structure of the company such as short-term joint ventures to accommodate demand.

Risk

If the economic data indicates that your firm's value will decline or not grow as forecasted, a risk has been identified. The risks to the viability of the business will gauge a company's response to economic issues. If the risk is high, a company must respond by strategic repositioning. For example, significant declines in prices may portend overheated competition in a particular marketplace. Is this a structural change in the

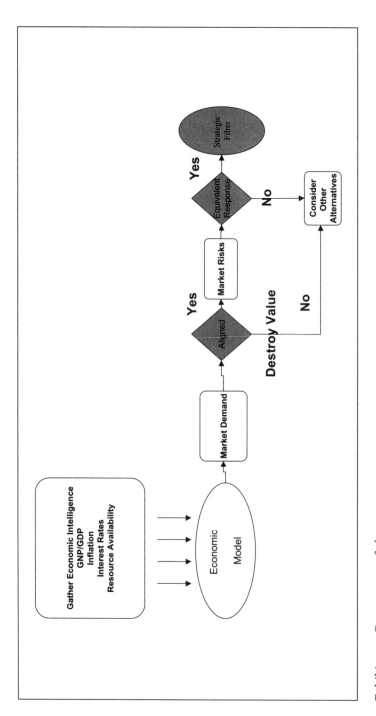

Exhibit 4-1. Permanency of change.

pricing dynamics of the marketplace? Is the market becoming more volatile? Will this lead to long-term erosion of profits and shareholder value? If the answer to the majority of these questions is yes, then choosing Strategic Alternatives that change your company's market position is appropriate. This may call for an overhaul of your business model, or an acquisition of competitors.

Strategic Alternatives that overcompensate for change will destroy value. A drastic change to a business model may be costly and difficult to implement. Dedication to attainable and forward-thinking goals creates competitive advantages. New initiatives need to be realistic and require careful coordination with the strategic, financial, and operating plans. Since competitive advantages are not permanent, how long will the advantage exist?

Conclusion

This chapter discussed the economic filter in the Step-Wise Approach to Value. The economic filter is the first screen that is used for evaluating Strategic Alternatives. This filter has a two-step process:

1) Understanding market demand

2) Validating the SA in connection with market demand

Market demand is simply the product price multiplied by the number of buyers. Market demand can be predicted using numerous economic factors. We discussed some common economic metrics such as GNP, GDP, inflation, interest rates, and resource availability. These metrics can serve as inputs to a market demand model.

With an understanding of the future direction of market demand, you can validate the SA by assessing its alignment with the market and its equivalence of action with market risks (Exhibit 4-2). Alignment with market demand tests how well a SA captures market demand. Equivalence of response gauges whether the SA addresses market risk appropriately. Market risk is the probability of not achieving the target shareholder value. If the alternative is aligned with market demand, achieves equivalence of response, and addresses market risk appropriately, then the SA should be tested using the strategic filter.

Notes

1. U.S. Department of Commerce, Bureau of Economic Analysis.
2. Ibid.

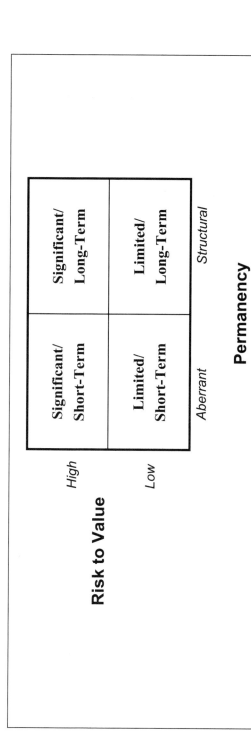

Exhibit 4-2. Characteristics for evaluating equivalence of action in Strategic Alternatives.

CHAPTER 5

The Strategic Filter

THE STRATEGIC FILTER is the second screen for evaluating Strategic Alternatives (SAs) in the Step-Wise Approach to Value (SWAV). In Chapter 4 we discussed the economic filter, which looks at an SA from the demand perspective. The take-away from the economic filter is that you know that you have sufficient market demand to support an SA and that it can provide equivalence of action. The next logical step is to validate whether the SA creates a competitive advantage. This validation occurs by first performing a strategic analysis—identifying competitive weaknesses and determining if the value proposition offsets the weaknesses.

This chapter discusses two tools, the Porter Model and the Balanced Scorecard, that can be used to analyze strategy. The tools are used to determine areas of improvement in your competitive position. Enhancement in these areas should result in a stronger competitive advantage. We will look at the competitive factors from an industry perspective using the Porter Model. This model analyzes change within an industry based on five forces: rivalry among competitors, pressure from buyers, pressure from suppliers, barriers to entry, and substitute products. The Balanced Scorecard brings nonfinancial metrics into the analytical tool kit. We will describe how the Balanced Scorecard is a central framework for assessing your strategy. The Balanced Scorecard takes a company-specific perspective that stresses measurement of four key quadrants: financial, customer, internal business process, and learning and growth.

Introduction to the Strategic Filter

The following consulting experience demonstrates the importance of this screen. We were engaged to assist with a merger integration of two financial services companies. The scope of our work was to evaluate the resource capabilities of a specific division.

The transaction had already been consummated,

and the value proposition communicated to the investment community was that the merger would result in increased revenue and improved efficiency. The acquiring company felt the merger would give it a stronger presence in two major metropolitan markets, with the ability to increase revenue. The revenue lift would be an increase over the combined revenues of both entities. It also felt that it could reduce expenses by consolidating branches and administrative functions in accounting, marketing, and human resources. The acquiring company was no stranger to M&A. It had made numerous acquisitions of numerous smaller competitors over a number of years, but this was by far the largest acquisition. In the past, the acquiring company was able to increase sales in new markets, through the use of aggressive pricing strategies. In our conversations with the executives, they indicated that they felt a similar strategy was the key to success with this merger. The company would use its increased presence and lower prices to boost revenue. Yet this strategy was not viable in the major markets that were targeted. There were numerous competitors with much greater pricing power that already had a significant presence in these markets. The combined company struggled to increase revenues. This resulted in the departure of the CEO. How does all of this demonstrate the importance of the strategic filter? Had the due diligence team focused on the strategic issues, more specifically the competitive rivalry in the target markets, they would have seen that the value proposition from the merger would not deliver shareholder value.

The Porter Model

The Porter Model is a conceptual framework used to understand what makes industry change. The model was developed by Michael E. Porter, a professor at Harvard Business School. The model facilitates the formation of business strategy through analysis of the five forces that drive and shape industries (Exhibit 5-1). Determining how these forces can change your business helps you identify your strategic weaknesses and improve your competitive advantage.

Intensity of Rivalry Among Competitors

Competitive intensity is dependent on the number and magnitude of actions taken by market players. Competitive actions can take many forms, such as changes in price, service, and quality. More actions and reactions to competitive movements intensify the amount of competition. Intensity may also be fueled by a few but significant actions, such as dramatic drops in price. Intensity of rivalry is also affected by industry growth rates, product type, the nature of the players, fixed or storage cost levels, and exit barriers.

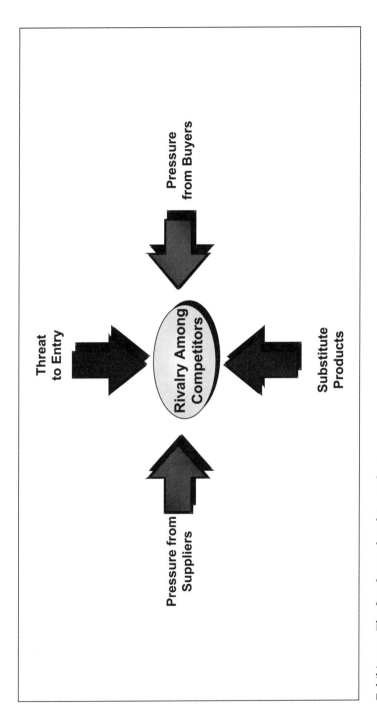

Exhibit 5-1. The five forces that drive industry.

❏ *Growth Rates.* This aspect of competitive intensity
is partially addressed in the economic filter, which
addresses changes in market demand. The economic filter assesses alignment with market demand
and impact. The focus here is on competition. For
purposes of the SWAV, we need to isolate how the
Strategic Alternatives will be affected by market
growth rates. In high-growth industries, business
performance can improve by keeping pace with the
market. Assuming a company is growing as fast as
its industry, it should increase in profits and size
with the market. Shareholder value will be driven
by a firm's membership in the industry. A slow-
growth environment will force its players to focus
on market share and efficiency to enhance shareholder value. The key to growth is to take market
share from other competitors, or to buy market
share by acquisition. The only way to increase
sales faster than the industry is to get your competitors' business. Increase in profits will come from
doing things more efficiently.

❏ *Product Type.* If the product is a commodity, the
industry players will compete on price. The major
characteristic of a commodity-driven marketplace
is that product functions and features of equal
quality can be delivered by the majority of the
competitors in the marketplace. Brand, customer
service, and customer loyalty are not major factors
in the buying decision. Oil, steel, and agriculture

can be categorized as commodity industries. This fuels more intense competition and tends to reduce the number of competitors. Markets that have complex products generate rivalry through differentiating product features and functions. Biotechnology is an example of an industry where products are highly differentiated.

❐ *The Nature of the Players.* The nature of the market players is a function of their comparative size, demographics, and strategy. Markets containing players of the same size tend to have more intense competition. The absence of a dominant player fuels intensity. Companies take more risks because of the limited impact of competitor responses on their business. Intensity wanes as dominant players emerge. Smaller firms may fear that retaliation by big players will put them out of business.

Market player strategy has an important role in competitive rivalry. If the success of a company is defined by its accomplishment in a particular industry, competition will intensify. This creates a "succeed at all costs" mentality. This strategy may be destructive when large companies are vying for market position.

❐ *Fixed/Storage Cost Levels.* High fixed costs increase competitive rivalry, usually in the form of price wars. This is caused by the push to fill existing capacity and to break even. The marketplace has a "ratchet-like" response to increased capacity (Exhibit 5-2). When capacity is added in large increments (i.e., businesses build large plants), competition tends to intensify. Capacity spikes lead to sharp price drops as businesses push to fill excess capacity. After the industry has reached an equilibrium point, intensity diminishes. This competitive lull will be interrupted by the next addition of a large increment of capacity.

❏ *Exit Barriers.* The steeper the exit barrier, the more intense the level of competition. If the cost of leaving a market is formidable, then firms tend to stay in the business. This may relate to selling special use assets, union contracts, or synergies with other operating divisions. Back to the example above, if a company has a significant investment in plants, they have created a barrier to exit. The barriers relate to sale of the plant and redeployment of workers and the time involved in liquidation, among other things.

Threat to Entry

Porter states that when barriers to entry are high, the danger of new competition breaking into the market diminishes. The threat from outside competition coming into the market is related to the six barriers to entry in the marketplace: economies of scale, product

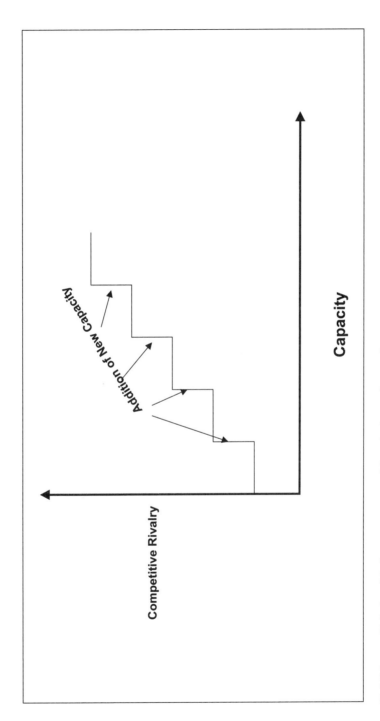

Exhibit 5-2. Relationship between competitive rivalry and capacity.

differentiation, switching costs, access to distribution channels, cost disadvantages independent of scale, and government policy.

❑ *Economies of Scale.* This barrier is established when market participants can produce a product less expensively than market newcomers. Economies of scale refer to the decrease in unit cost as the volume produced increases. Exhibit 5-3 illustrates the relationship between production level and unit cost. If ABC Corp. is entering the market and chooses to produce 10,000 units, the cost of production is $110 per unit. At a production level of 20,000, the unit cost declines to sixty dollars. The cost advantage of a 20,000-unit production level over a 10,000-unit level is fifty dollars per unit. The significance of economies of scale diminishes as production levels increase. When ABC doubles production from 50,000 to 100,000 units, they would only realize a decline in unit cost of ten dollars, as shown in Exhibit 5-3.

The economics of scale issue creates three choices for the newcomer:

1. Enter the market on a very large scale to be price-competitive. (This requires a significant investment.)

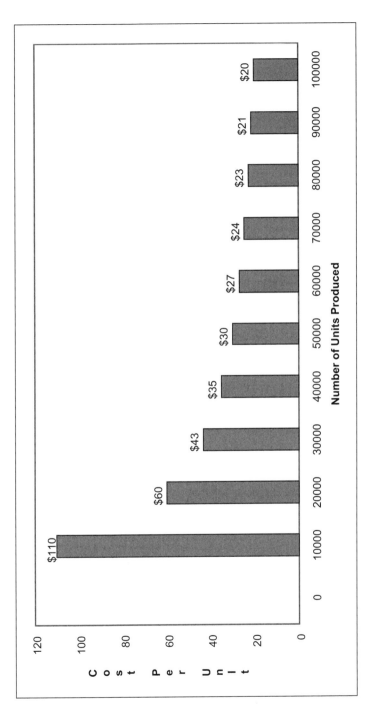

Exhibit 5-3. ABC Corp. unit costs.

2. Make a limited investment and operate at a cost disadvantage.

3. Identify a strategic partner with manufacturing capability and share potential profits.

❐ *Product Differentiation.* When entering a new market, a company may encounter competitors who have achieved customer loyalty through advertising, customer service, and a prior market presence. It then becomes crucial for the new company to differentiate its product from those of its competitors.

❐ *Switching Costs.* Entering into new markets may require new supplier relationships. These costs are incurred when changing from one supplier to another. For example, entry into the equipment rental business by an equipment manufacturer may require new inventory-tracking software. The switching costs in this instance are:

Switching Cost	Example
Employee retraining costs	Training employees on new software
Costs of new ancillary equipment	Purchasing new hardware to run the software
Cost in time and system testing	Time expended by the information technology staff

Psychic costs   Staff-related issues
                                 around operation of
                                 the new software and
                                 difficulty with interac-
                                 tion with outside staff

❏ *Access to Distribution Channels.* Developing distribution channels for new products is difficult and
   may require special incentives. A distribution
   channel is a method of getting product to market.
   For example, in the retail industry, the distribution
   channel consists of direct sales to your customer
   (such as the Gateway stores where customers buy
   PCs directly from Gateway Computers). Established market participants have the advantage of
   existing platforms to market products. Channel
   partners, such as distributors, may view existing
   relationships as less risky. E-commerce has improved access to distribution channels by creating
   product exchanges and marketplaces. In addition,
   e-commerce has inherent barriers that are technological and not physical. For example, a company
   may encounter problems in getting software systems from different companies to interact with one
   another.

❏ *Cost Disadvantages Independent of Scale.* Existing
   competitors also have advantages over new market
   players that stem from the following four factors:

1. Proprietary product technology such as patents, trademarks, or internal processes. (Viagra is an example here.)

2. Favorable access to raw materials from purchasing agreements with suppliers. (This is a major cost advantage.)

3. Favorable locations that are more accessible to raw materials, or within closer proximity of customers and/or destination. (Hotels located close to beaches or ski slopes are one example.)

4. Better-trained management and staff. (This constitutes a learning or experience curve that has already been traveled.)

❑ *Government Policy.* The government may create barriers to market entry to assure the welfare of its citizens, or to constrain growth of business. Two policies that serve as obstacles to entering a marketplace are:

1. Licensing requirements that local governments have enacted. (An example is the licensing requirement for selling alcoholic beverages.)

2. Limits to access of raw materials. (The paper industry has limited access to national forests constraining logging for environmental purposes.)

Bargaining Power of Suppliers

High supplier bargaining power constrains market participants' ability to negotiate pricing, quality, and service. As supplier power increases, industry profit margins will decline because costs will increase. Companies are unable to pass price increases on to customers, as customers become price-sensitive. In the mid-nineties, gasoline retailers were affected by the power that oil refiners had to increase the cost of gasoline. The comparable size between the supplier and the buyer plays a role in this relationship. If the suppliers are larger than the buyers, they tend to have a higher degree of bargaining power. A small, family-run gas station being supplied by a large oil company is an example of this relationship. Since the family-run business is at the behest of a few large suppliers, the bargaining power of the supplying oil companies is greater.

Bargaining Power of Buyers

The ability of the buyer to negotiate the terms of sale significantly affects pricing and profits. As the customer becomes more powerful, downward pressure is exerted on pricing and profitability. Customer service begins to improve as industry participants find different ways to compete. Improved service has been observed in the banking industry as deregulation and overcapacity has pushed banks to compress product delivery times. Banks have dropped loan approval time from one week to one day on many types of commercial loans.

Substitute Products

Items that decrease sales of products within an industry are substitute products. For example, frozen yogurt is considered a substitute for ice cream. Sport utility vehicles (SUVs) can be considered a substitute product to the automobile. Substitutes can be viewed in two ways. They can be viewed negatively by the industry because they siphon off revenue from auto sales.

The other perspective is that substitute products add to the breadth of the industry by creating opportunities that increase the overall market. Auto companies have enjoyed higher profits because the SUVs have higher margins. This has prompted Mercedes Benz to widen its product offering to include this type of vehicle.

Using the Porter Model to Drive Value

The Porter Model provides an industry view of the business. The strength of the model is that it identifies where a firm must improve its competitive position. This model forces you to identify your competitors and benchmark your company against your competition, suppliers, and buyers. This comparative analysis will result in areas of competitive strengths and weaknesses. It also causes management to understand its position in the value chain.

Exhibit 5-4 depicts the value chain and comparative characteristics that can be used to compare buyers and suppliers. A value or supply chain places your company on a continuum between suppliers or the purveyors of resources to your company and buyers or your customers. Bargaining power can be determined by comparing company size, number of suppliers/buyers, financial condition, substitutes available, and product differentiation. Superior size and financial position, as well as a limited number of buyers or suppliers, tend to improve bargaining power. If there are substitute products available, the bargaining power of the supplier will erode. If your firm is in an industry where substitute products are available, your bargaining power will decrease. The possession of products that are differentiated tends to increase the bargaining power of suppliers and the bargaining power of your firm in selling to your buyers.

The strength of the Porter Model lies in its identification of threats to entry and substitute products that managers can use to identify weaknesses in their existing strategies. Management may decide to shift

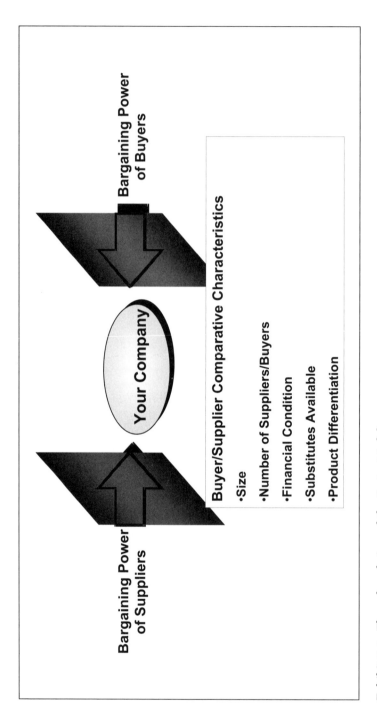

Exhibit 5-4. The value chain and the Porter Model.

market position, channels, or its customers, based on pressures from the five forces. The weakness of the model is that it is industry-specific. This can tend to create industry myopia. Executives can be overly focused on industry pressures and not look outside their own competitive space for different ways of doing business. Many standards for customer service are often set outside particular industries. For example, customer service expectations set by catalog retailer Lands' End have been imposed on other industries like insurance.

The Balanced Scorecard

Robert S. Kaplan and David P. Norton developed the Balanced Scorecard. It was designed to more effectively turn strategic plans into action. The scorecard creates a way to measure performance in strategic terms. It is not only a way to benchmark the performance of a company, but it is a process as well. The scorecard involves continual evaluation of four key areas, or quadrants, as well as assessment of the actual metrics themselves. The process occurs at all levels of management. The four quadrants are financial, customer, internal business process, and learning and growth, which were identified by Kaplan and Norton as areas that are key to business success (Exhibit 5-5).

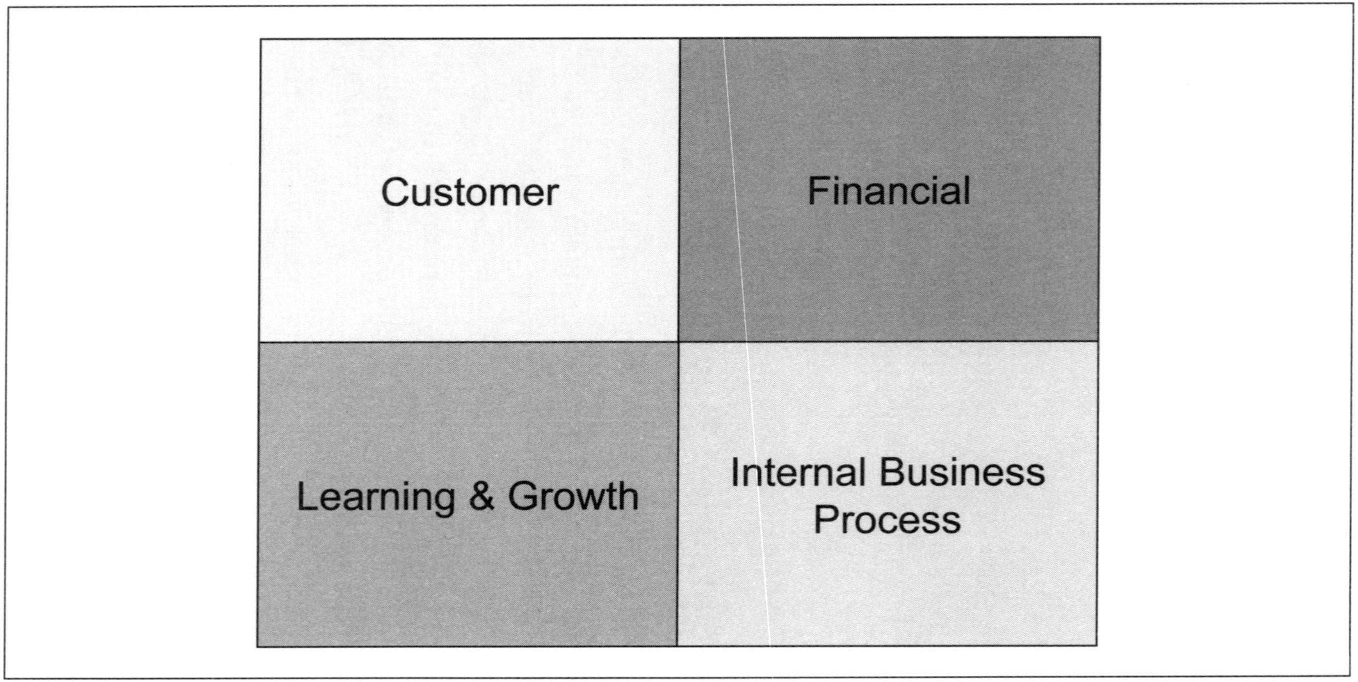

Exhibit 5-5. The Balanced Scoreboard.

The Financial Quadrant

The financial quadrant of the scorecard measures performance in three major categories: 1) revenue growth, 2) productivity, and 3) return on investment. These categories are linked to the maturity of your business. The maturity of a business closely parallels the development of industries. Jackson proposes three stages of the industry lifecycle.[1] Financial metrics are summarized in Exhibit 5-6.

❐ *Pioneer.* This is the nascent stage of an industry, characterized by high growth in revenues and heavy investment. The Internet sector in the late 1990s is representative of this stage. During this time period, thousands of websites were launched and investment capital was flooding in from private and public sources. Some examples of metrics used to measure financial success are percentage revenue growth, revenue per employee, and revenue turnover (revenue/assets).

❐ *Expansion.* As initial growth moderates, industries move into the expansion phase. The financial focus begins to shift toward earnings. The inflow of capital declines as the markets recognize that the prospect of meteoric growth is no longer possible. Performance indicators that are useful in this stage are revenue from specific markets, profit per employee, and return on assets.

Metric	Pioneer	Expansion	Stabilization
Revenue Growth	% Revenue Growth	Revenue by Market	Revenue by Product
Productivity	Revenue per Employee	Profit per Employee	Unit Cost
ROI	Revenue Turnover (Revenue/Assets)	Return on Assets	Return on Equity

Exhibit 5-6. Financial quadrant representative metrics.

❏ *Stabilization.* In this stage, growth becomes comparable to the economy as a whole and improvement in earnings is driven by productivity and management of costs. The emphasis begins to shift toward measurement of earnings and return on equity. Management emphasizes cost control and minimizing the capital required to run the business. Measurements used for financial success in the stabilization stage include revenue by product, unit cost, and return on equity.

The Customer Quadrant

Businesses that do not understand their customers and markets will ultimately fail. The core measurements in this group are shown in Exhibit 5-7, with respective examples based on a community bank.

The Internal Business Process Quadrant

Kaplan segments business processes into three basic categories: 1) innovation, 2) production, and 3) post-sale service. Exhibit 5-8 shows metrics that can be used to measure the contribution of these processes to shareholder value.

Measurement	Definition	Metric
Market Share	The percentage of sales that a company holds in a specific market	% of total loan volume generated by small business in the community area
Customer Acquisition	The number of new customers a company obtains in a specific time period	Ratio of new customers to existing customers in a year
Customer Satisfaction	The overall customer affinity for goods or services delivered by a company.	Index of satisfaction based on survey on results (opinion of branch experiences, rating of Web-based services and call center)
Customer Profitability	Profit measured on a customer by customer basis	Total income less cost of sales products and service on a per customer basis (See Chapter 8 on Activity-Based Management for details)

Exhibit 5-7. Customer quadrant measurements.

Process	Function	Metric
Innovation	Strategy	Revenue Growth
	Product Development	Revenue from New Products
Operations	Manufacturing	Cost per unit
	Delivery	Average Delivery Time
Post Sale Service	Customer	Satisfaction Index

Exhibit 5-8. Internal business process metrics.

The Learning and Growth Quadrant

"The objectives of the learning and growth perspective provide the infrastructure to enable ambitious objectives in the other three perspectives to be achieved."[2] Kaplan and Cooper believe that this area is the key to long-term growth. This quadrant is centered around three areas: 1) employee capabilities, 2) information system capabilities, and 3) motivation, empowerment, and alignment. As mentioned throughout this book, these areas have been overlooked in the past because they have not shown tangible contributions to the bottom line. Lack of attention to learning and growth is similar to avoiding regular maintenance and repair on your home. Initially, the effects will not be readily apparent, but may over time build to dramatic proportions. Just like a small water leak can destroy a wall, lack of alignment (goal sharing) and motivation will have devastating effects on a company's ability to be productive and generate shareholder value. Unfortunately, these areas are the most difficult to measure. Organizational constructs are difficult for traditionally trained managers to understand. Managers have a high degree of comfort with "hard" metrics such as time, costs, and revenues. These can be tied directly into the financial performance of the company. It is difficult to link employee satisfaction with cost control or sales. These relationships are anecdotal at best; for example, "Disgruntled employees will not treat your customers well because they are unhappy."

Some of the same conceptual fuzziness with learning and growth is prevalent in evaluating technology. Assessing the performance of the technological infrastructure can be straightforward (e.g., system downtime). The challenge arises when trying to understand how well technology meets the requirements of the business. Exhibit 5-9 shows metrics for the learning and growth quadrant.

Using the Balanced Scorecard to Drive Value

In summary, the Balanced Scorecard enhances shareholder value through measurement and action in four areas: financial, customer, internal business process,

Area of Focus	Measurement Target	Metric
Employee Capabilities	Satisfaction	Satisfaction Index (1)
	Retention	Turnover Rate
	Productivity	Net Income per Employee
Information Systems	Technology Platform	Availability, Reliability, Scalability
	Software	Ability to Perform Functional Requirements
	Database	Ability to Capture Customer Experience
Organizational Alignment & Motivation	Motivation	Cultural Climate
	Strategic Alignment	Goodness of Fit to Departmental Goals

(1) Composite Index of employee attitudes concerning work environment, management practices, benefits, and work hours, among other things

(2) Composite index of employee alignment with mission and values of the company

Exhibit 5-9. Learning and growth metrics.

and learning and growth. Action takes the form of new initiatives that are developed by specific strategies in the four areas or quadrants. It also recognizes foundational business components that are essential for the long-term growth of the business. Research has found that a higher percentage of measurement-managed companies were identified as industry leaders, as being financially in the top third of their industry, and as successfully managing their change effort.

The Balanced Scorecard has three major strengths. First, it creates measurements that can be used to manage and guide an organization. Second, the Balanced Scorecard makes an effort to measure some soft factors such as customer satisfaction and organizational alignment. Third, the framework can be used to create a process to manage strategy. This provides a way for the strategy to be implemented into business operations. The major weakness of this measurement system is that it does not link to valuation metrics. We will discuss the valuation filter in Chapter 11.

Conclusion

In conclusion, this chapter discussed the strategic filter of the Step-Wise Approach to Value. Two tools can be used to make this assessment, the Porter Model and the Balanced Scorecard. The Porter Model identifies how industry forces impact the business. These forces are: 1) competitive rivalry, 2) pressure from suppliers, 3) pressure from buyers, 4) substitute products, and 5) threat of entry. Its strengths lie in the discipline it creates to benchmark your company to its competitors, buyers, and suppliers and to identify competitive threats and substitute products. Its weakness is that the model is industry-focused and does not look outside your particular industry for new ideas.

The Balanced Scorecard creates a measurement system used to monitor and create strategy. It looks at strategy from a more focused perspective in that it takes a company-specific view. The scorecard for a company should measure success in the following areas: 1) financial, 2) customer, 3) internal business process, and 4) learning and growth. The measurement and process orientation of the Balanced Scorecard are its greatest strengths. The problem with the scorecard is that it does not use value-driven metrics to measure the effectiveness of strategy.

Both tools are widely accepted methods of understanding business strategy. The selection of a tool is driven by the best fit of the method to your business and which tool provides you with an understanding of how to improve your company's competitive advantage.

Notes

1. Charles P. Jones, *Investments, Analyses, and Interpretation, 7th Edition* (New York: Wiley & Sons, 2000), pp. 369–371.
2. Robert S. Kaplan and David P. Norton, *The Balanced Scorecard: Translating Strategy into Action* (Boston: Harvard Business School Press, 1996), p. 126.

PART 3

The Operational Filter

CHAPTER 6

Introduction to the Operational Filter

THE NEXT TWO CHAPTERS (Chapter 7 and Chapter 8) will discuss the operational filter of the Step-Wise Approach to Value (SWAV). The purpose of this filter is to understand how a Strategic Alternative (SA) impacts the financial performance of a company. Many companies perform an analysis on a strategic alternative in isolation. That is, they look at the incremental increase in value that a SA would potentially generate. This type of analysis looks at cash flow improvements that are mostly generated in later years. What it fails to take into consideration is the short-term impacts on the financial performance of a company, as well as the potential destruction of value from interactive effects.

Short-term impacts on financial performance may include increases in costs (such as implementation costs) and/or productivity losses. Many business executives fail to see the short-term destruction of value from SAs. Companies that are looking to increase revenues and that are involved in merger and acquisition (M&A) activity may find that sales from the acquired company are going down and not up. This may be caused by cannibalization of revenue from other channels. What the merger has created is internal competition for revenue (as opposed to external competition) resulting in lower and not higher sales. Cannibalization may also occur when electronic sales channels are introduced. Many companies thought that launching websites would increase sales. What they discovered is that customers switched from traditional channels (like buying products in stores) to buying products over the Internet. In addition, cash flow may decrease if the acquiring company borrows excessively to make the acquisition. Many leveraged buyouts that were structured in the 1980s failed because the debt-laden acquisitions could not handle the excessive interest payments.

How does the operational filter detect short-term impacts and interactive effects? A number of financial tools are used to detect these erosive effects. The Du-Pont Model is a diagnostic tool that looks at the components of return on assets and return on equity to determine if changes in the income statement and/or the capital structure (the mix of debt and equity used to finance operations) are affecting financial performance. Activity-based management looks at the profit and cost structure of an organization based on the processes it performs.

Now that we tested the Strategic Alternative with the economic and strategic filters, we move to the operational aspect of the Step-Wise Approach to Value. We will discuss a number of tools used to analyze financial performance. We will show how to measure management performance (using the DuPont Model). We will look at what drives shareholder returns: profit margins, efficient utilization of assets, and leverage. We will show you how to assess your management of 1) the income statement to increase profit margins and 2) the balance sheet to increase asset turnover (utilization of assets). By understanding these tools you will be in a position to increase return on assets. We will also show how the use of leverage (change in the amount of debt used to finance corporate investments) can impact return to shareholders.

We will also describe the use of activity-based costing to obtain meaningful information for decision making. Most financial reporting systems and standard costing systems simply don't do the job, particularly in today's competitive environment. They look backward and are general ledger– and transaction-orientated. Accordingly, we will focus on the application of ABC/ABM models to quantify resources consumed and the real cost of each activity. We will also look at the estimation of the true costs of production and the determination of real, measurable benefits.

Examination of operational drivers is key in addressing both short- and long-term impacts of Strategic Alternatives on shareholder value.

CHAPTER 7

The DuPont Model

Introduction to the DuPont Model

THE PURPOSE of this chapter is to discuss the Du-Pont Model and its use in the operational filter. This model has been used to detect the drivers of change in financial performance. The model is also an excellent tool for a forward-looking assessment of Strategic Alternatives. The DuPont Model was originally developed in 1919 by a finance executive at E.I. du Pont de Nemours and Co. of Wilmington, Delaware, for financial planning and control purposes. The DuPont system helps many companies understand the critical

149

building blocks in return on assets (ROA) and return on equity (ROE).

Return on assets is a measure of the productivity of assets. Assets appear on your balance sheet. They are things that you own. Some examples of assets are equipment, real estate, inventory, software, trademarks, and patents. ROA tells you how much net income your assets are generating. This type of measurement is important in understanding short-run impacts to value. It can be used to measure the productivity of Strategic Alternatives in isolation and combined with the rest of the business. ROA is an important tool for the analysis of mergers and acquisitions because it measures the productivity of the transaction on the total purchase price.

Return on equity (ROE) measures productivity in relation to equity. This measure focuses on the part of the investment that is funded by equity. Strategic Alternatives can be funded using two sources: debt and equity. Debt is money that is borrowed (for example, money from the bank). Equity is money that is contributed by shareholders. Projects are funded using a mix of debt and equity. This mix affects the cost of capital, which may be used as the adjustment for time and risk (as discussed in Chapter 10)—more specifically, the risk adjustment. Risk adjustments start with a benchmark called the cost of capital that takes into account the proportions of debt and equity used to fund a Strategic Alternative. A detailed treatment of the cost of capital can be found in Chapter 10.

By virtue of its familiarity and simplicity, the Du-Pont Model is a way of visualizing the components of ROA and ROE. A typical DuPont chart resembles a chart drawn to mark the progress of competitors in a tennis or basketball tournament, as shown in Exhibit 7-1. This schematic shows how the formula links all aspects of the balance sheet and income statement together.

An alternate and more brief form of the DuPont approach is to use the formula itself where ROA and ROE are broken down into their component parts for further analysis, as shown in Exhibit 7-2.

These components are the drivers of financial performance and consequently intrinsic value. In order to use this model to evaluate SAs, we need to adjust the model to align with the intrinsic value model. Our concept of value is based on cash flow and not net income. The difference between cash flow and net income is that cash flow does not contain noncash charges (such as depreciation, amortization, and depletion) that distort operating performance of current periods. This adjustment makes the formula appear as follows in Exhibit 7-3.

Before we use the model in its new form, we need to spend time understanding its specific components.

Cash Flow Margin

The cash flow margin shows you the relationship between your cost structure and your revenue stream.

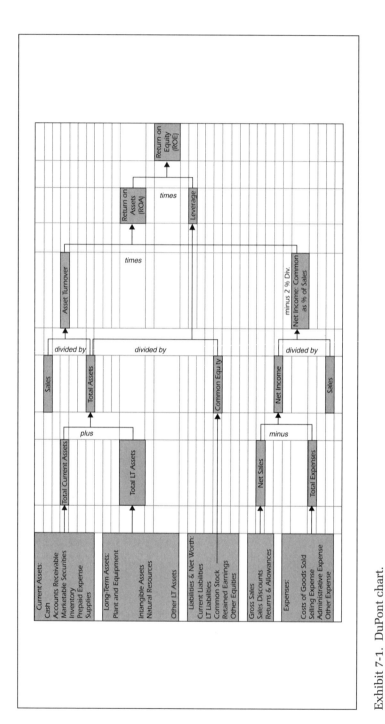

Exhibit 7-1. DuPont chart.

Profit Margin	×	Asset Turnover	=	Return on Assets (ROA)
$\dfrac{\text{Net income}}{\text{Sales}}$	×	$\dfrac{\text{Sales}}{\text{Total assets}}$	=	$\dfrac{\text{Net income}}{\text{Total assets}}$
Return on Assets (ROA)	×	Financial Leverage	=	Return on Equity (ROE)
$\dfrac{\text{Net income}}{\text{Total assets}}$	×	$\dfrac{\text{Total assets}}{\text{Common equity}}$	=	$\dfrac{\text{Net income}}{\text{Common equity}}$

Exhibit 7-2. DuPont chart—alternate version.

Cash Flow Margin	×	Asset Turnover	=	Adjusted Return on Assets (ROA)
$\dfrac{\text{Cash flow}}{\text{Sales}}$	×	$\dfrac{\text{Sales}}{\text{Total assets}}$	=	$\dfrac{\text{Cash flow}}{\text{Total assets}}$
Adjusted Return on Assets (ROA)	×	Financial Leverage	=	Adjusted Return on Equity (ROE)
$\dfrac{\text{Cash flow}}{\text{Total assets}}$	×	$\dfrac{\text{Total assets}}{\text{Common equity}}$	=	$\dfrac{\text{Cash flow}}{\text{Common equity}}$

Exhibit 7-3. Adjusted DuPont chart.

This is an indicator of how well an operation is being managed. High cash flow margins are indicative of two things: a high price environment and/or an efficient operation. Let's assume you are looking at a merger of equals with a competitor. Assume the value proposition is to increase revenue and cash flow. What are the impacts to the productivity of your assets overall? Assume that the merger would result in higher short-term costs that would decrease your cash flow margin by 2 percent. The short-term decline in ROA is 8 percent if the ratio between sales and assets is held constant (Exhibit 7-4). The question you need to ask yourself is whether the spike in costs is short-term. In this case, we are trading a revenue increase for efficiency.

Asset Turnover

This component of the DuPont Model looks at the productivity of your assets to generate revenue. Asset turnover judges the ability of your assets to produce revenue. Many mergers are predicated on cleaning up the balance sheet of the acquired company. This is a euphemism for selling off assets that do not produce revenue. Assume that you are getting a good price for a company, but it will reduce your asset turnover from 4 to 3.5. The impact to ROA is illustrated in Exhibit 7-5.

The result is a drop of 6 percent in ROA. The question you need to ask is: Can you sell the assets off, or will they remain on your balance sheet?

	Cash Flow Margin	×	Asset Turnover	=	Adjusted ROA
Your Company	12%	×	4	=	48%
Combined Companies	10%	×	4	=	40%

Exhibit 7-4. Effect of a decrease in cash flow margin on return on assets.

	Cash Flow Margin	×	Asset Turnover	=	Adjusted ROA
Your Company	12%	×	4	=	48%
Combined Companies	12%	×	3.5	=	42%

Exhibit 7-5. Effect of a decrease in asset turnover on return on assets.

A Combination of Factors

Realistically, what would the ROA change be? It would be a combination of both a decrease in the cash flow margin and asset turnover. If the impacts we described above were combined, the result would look something like Exhibit 7-6.

The result is a decline of 13 percent in ROA. Drops in ROA are a normal short-run occurrence in M&A activity.

Financial Leverage

Financial leverage is the relationship between total assets and equity or shareholder investment. It mea-

	Cash Flow Margin	×	Asset Turnover	=	Adjusted ROA
Your Company	12%	×	4	=	48%
Combined Companies	10%	×	3.5	=	35%

Exhibit 7-6. Effect of a decrease in both cash flow margin and asset turnover on return on assets.

sures the amount of equity that is used to acquire assets. If leverage is high, then a limited amount of equity is used to buy assets. This means that the primary source of financing is debt. If the financial leverage is low, then more equity is used to buy assets. What are the implications from a shareholder value perspective? Risk to shareholders increase as they invest more in a business. Hence investors will demand a larger return for the increase in risk. This will tend to increase the cost of capital that will be used to adjust cash flows to arrive at an intrinsic value.

On the other hand, the use of debt can have a significant impact on value. Debt gives rise to interest charges that will reduce cash flow. Excessive amounts of debt can offset cash flow gains if interest payments exceed the benefits generated by the Strategic Alternative. Increases in leverage can be a leading indicator of erosion of value, if debt is managed improperly.

How does this help evaluate SAs? A quick look at leverage can tell us if the risk profile is changing. If leverage is the driver in increasing ROE, then the change in value is not due to the SA, but how it is being financed.

A Comprehensive Example

To illustrate how the DuPont Model is used, let's use the following hypothetical balance sheet and income statement figures from a company we will call Cobain Enterprises (Exhibit 7-7 and Exhibit 7-8, respectively).

Let's work through an example of how a hypothetical SA will affect ROA using DuPont. Assume that Cobain is looking to implement a $25 million supply chain management technology. Assume the following changes to the financial statement (Exhibit 7-9).

❏ Fixed assets will increase by $20 million for the acquisition of the software and hardware associated with the system. The depreciation and amortization is $5 million per year over a five-year life. Depreciation and amortization would reduce the value of the assets. Total assets would become $2,263 million (total assets of $2,243 million plus $25 million, less $5 million in amortization and depreciation).

❏ Assume a cash flow improvement of $9 million (see Exhibit 10-3 in Chapter 10 for details). Remember that this is a model that measures short-term impacts, so we can include these costs, assuming that they may not be incurred in future periods.

Exhibit 7-9 shows an increase in adjusted ROA from 6.5 percent to 6.8 percent. After looking at the

Average 2004	$ Millions	% to Sales
Accts. receivable	140	2.0
Inventory	1,235	7.8
Other current assets	107	1.5
Total current assets	1,482	21.3
Less current liabilities	(1,256)	18.1
Equals working capital	226	3.3
Net fixed assets	2,017	29.0
Total assets	2,243	32.3
LT liabilities	1,266	18.2
Preferred stock	255	3.7
Common equity	722	10.3
Total liabilities plus equity	2,243	32.3

Year Ended 12/31/2001	$ Millions	% to Sales
Net Sales	6,945	100.0%
Gross margin	1,672	24.1%
Operating expenses	1,460	21.0%
Operating profit	212	3.1%
Depreciation and amortization	40	0.6%
Interest	65	0.9%
Other income	8	0.1%
Income before tax	155	2.2%
Income taxes	50	0.7%
Net income	105	1.5%
Depreciation and amortization	40	0.6%
Cash flow*	145	2.1%

*Cash flow = net income + depreciation

Exhibit 7-7. Cobain Enterprises's balance sheet.

	Cash Flow Margin	×	Asset Turnover	=	Return on Assets (ROA)
Calculations	$\dfrac{145}{6,945}$	×	$\dfrac{6,945}{2,243}$	=	$\dfrac{145}{2,243}$
	Adjusted Return on Assets (ROA)	×	Financial Lever-age	=	Return on Equity (ROE)
Percentage	2.1%	×	3.1	=	6.5%

Exhibit 7-8. Cobain's Coffee Roasters income statement.

	Cash Flow Margin	×	Asset Turnover	=	Adjusted Return on Assets (ROA)
Calculations	$\dfrac{154}{6,945}$	×	$\dfrac{6,945}{2,263}$	=	$\dfrac{154}{2,263}$
	Adjusted Return on Assets (ROA)	×	Financial Lever-age	=	Adjusted Return on Equity (ROE)
Percentage	2.2%	×	3.1	=	6.8%

Exhibit 7-9. Impact on the adjusted ROA.

drivers of ROA (cash flow margin and asset turnover), the impact to ROA comes from a lift in the cash flow margin. Asset turnover offsets the cash flow margin increase as it declines from 4.5 × sales to 4.4 × sales (× meaning "times").

Strengths of the DuPont Model

The main advantage of the DuPont Model is its simplicity. It reveals how the key ratios link with each other to govern total financial performance. The model gives you a look into important drivers of financial performance such as cash flow to revenues and asset turnover. It also enables one to ask "what if" kinds of strategic questions that help to gauge what kind of impact implementing changes can have.

Types of "what if" questions that the model can handle are:

1. After the acquisition of a small competitor, what will the ROA and ROE be?

2. What will the proposed upgrade to a new customer ordering system be on ROE?

3. If inventory turnover improves after implementations stemming from a nine-month re-engineering project, how much will improve ROA?

The DuPont model can be used to understand short-term performance and not long-term value. It is a strong screen to test for impacts to operational metrics, but not intrinsic value. In its unadjusted form (net income–based) it has less linkage to cash generation and is less indicative of value.

Conclusion

The DuPont Model is a tool that is used in the operational filter. Its function in the operational filter is to understand the short-term impacts on value. In other settings the model had been used to diagnose changes in ROA and ROE. The ROA model looks at two drivers of financial performance—profit margin and asset turnover. We have adjusted the model for our purposes to align with the concept of intrinsic value. We have replaced the profit margin with cash flow in the profit margin calculation to integrate the concept of cash flow into the model. This new component, called the cash flow margin, measures how efficiently a business is being managed. The other driver in the equation, asset turnover, is a gauge of the ability of your assets to produce revenue.

ROE integrates the concept of leverage into the ROA model. Leverage is the relationship between debt and equity. This relationship has an impact on the adjustment for risk (the cost of capital) in the intrinsic value formula. We will discuss this relationship in Chapter 10. ROE is an indication of how much cash flow your equity or shareholder investment is producing.

The DuPont concept is used in the SWAV to pinpoint short-term swings in ROA based on changes that Strategic Alternatives will make on business drivers. The critical point is to understand whether these short-term swings may become permanent changes in the company. It also is a way of doing "what if" scenarios quickly. The DuPont Model is a diagnostic tool and does not measure intrinsic value. It is focused on the short-term trends as opposed to long-term value.

CHAPTER 8

Activity-Based
Management

THE DUPONT MODEL assesses the impact of Strategic Alternatives (SAs) by analyzing drivers of financial performance. It provides a high-level view of drivers that affect financial performance. The next step in the operational filter of the Step-Wise Approach to Value (SWAV) is to evaluate SAs in terms of business processes. Activity-based management (ABM) helps you understand the process impacts of Strategic Alternatives.

This financial technique was developed in the

1980s by Robert Kaplan and Robin Cooper, Harvard Business School professors. The tool was initially developed as a way to understand resource consumption and was used as a costing tool called activity-based costing (ABC). It is prevalent in many Fortune 1000 companies (such as Mobil and Chrysler) and is different from traditional accounting methods because it is based on connecting costs to activities (how expenses are incurred)—not broad categories (what expenses are incurred on). Activity-based costing will partition these costs by specific processes (activities) and drive them into sales channels, customers, and units of production. Another variant to ABC is activity-based management or ABM. ABM is a management system that produces the profitability and costing data on a regular basis to drive decision making.

Attaching Costs to Your Business Process

ABM gives you the ability to attach costs to your business process. These costs can give you ideas about your process changes, core competencies, and strategic alternatives. Exhibit 8-1 illustrates an ABM analysis of an IT project.

The conventional method of understanding costs is depicted the left, and the ABM view of the project

Conventional vs. ABMBudgets

Conventional Mehtod	
Salaries and Bonuses	$1,800,000
Consulting Fees	$300,000
Software License Fees	$300,000
Communications Fees	$450,000
Hardware Vendor Maintenance Agreement	$150,000
Total	$3,000,000

ABM Method	
Develop Initiative Strategy & Planning	$150,000
Design and Implement	$600,000
Test & Deploy	$150,000
Operate Existing Systems	$900,000
Maint & Upgrade Systems	$1,200,000
Total	$3,000,000

Exhibit 8-1. An ABM analysis of an IT project.

is depicted on the right. Conventional financial reporting aggregates shared costs into categories based on what resources are, such as consulting fees and software fees. The ABM method takes a process view focusing on how money is being spent in processes like design and implementation. This enables you to weigh the cost versus the value of specific activities, processes, and tasks. A process question arising from the task view is, "Why are maintenance expenses consuming the majority of the initiative costs, and how can they be reduced?"

How does this help assess Strategic Alternatives? It gives management a financial measure that serves two purposes in assessing processes. First, you can attach a monetary value of a certain activity or task as a way to initiate process changes. If you are looking to reengineering to improve efficiency, ABM will identify areas of improvement. A certain activity can look overly expensive and may warrant further investigation. The activity view in Exhibit 8-2 shows us an example where $160,000 was spent on recruiting.

There may be two ways to lower this high cost: First, change the activity (redesign or reengineer the process) or change contiguous activities that may be driving these costs. Streamlining the number of candidate interviews with HR personnel is an example of an activity change. Developing a focused approach to staffing departments (to eliminate unneeded interviews and employee searches) illustrates a change to

Activity View			Finance & Accounting	Functional View	
Recruiting	$160,000	40%	Finance & Accounting	$40,000	10%
Benefits Administration	$40,000	10%	HR	$20,000	5%
Training	$80,000	20%	Manufacturing	$80,000	20%
Employee Remediation	$40,000	10%	Plant	$20,000	5%
Employee Relations	$80,000	20%	Information Technology	$240,000	60%
Total	$400,000	100%	Total	$400,000	100%

Exhibit 8-2. Human resources process.

a contiguous process. A second redesign alternative is to lower the cost of interview scheduling by hiring an administrator for $50,000 per year to handle scheduling, as opposed to having HR directors earning $120,000 per year handling this process. ABM lets you get to the heart of the process issues before spending a tremendous amount of time and effort to change processes that may already be financially efficient.

Second, you can assess the strategic value of an activity. The strategic view provides the information to assess the value of an activity against the core competencies of the company. The central question in this analysis becomes, "Is this activity worth the money we are currently paying to perform it?" If the answer to the question is no, then Strategic Alternatives can be considered to reduce cost.

Building an ABM Model

The high-level steps that are needed to create an ABM model are delineated below. The level of effort to perform an ABM study may range from days to years, contingent upon the level of complexity of the model and the organization. ABM is a directional tool and requires some judgment as to how the model is created. This type of judgment is a critical success factor for the ABM initiative. The level of detail must be sufficient to provide information to support strategic and operational analysis. On the other hand, complexity needs to be limited to keep costs down and make the model understandable for users who are not part of the tactical processes.

Step 1: Defining the End Result

The key to any successful project is to have a clear understanding of what the end result will look like. Successful implementation of ABM starts with understanding your objectives for the initiative. ABM models should be designed to answer critical questions about cost patterns in your organization.

The first task in an ABM project is to develop a matrix similar to Exhibit 8-3. This matrix captures the questions, the metric that answers the questions, and the category that will be answered by the study. These patterns can be divided into two categories: strategic and operational. Strategic items reveal insights into a company's customers, divisions, products, and units of production. Operational items provide vision into core processes. Robin Cooper states that ABM "software systems should be designed to support two separate systems, one for strategic costing and the other for operational improvement."[1] The separation of systems assures that each level of management gets the specific information required to make decisions.

Splitting systems functions creates a focus and mitigates risks associated with complexity.

Questions should come from numerous levels in the organization. There is usually a difference between what interests senior management and others in the company. It is valuable to capture and prioritize the needs of middle management here to enroll them in the process of building the model You will rely on them heavily to build the activity dictionary, select employees for data gathering, and validate the results. Exhibit 8-3 describes representative questions that ABM can answer. Questions like these will give you an idea of the structure, or architecture, of the ABM model. These systems should enable managers to make forward-thinking decisions, apply the specific operation, and link them together.

Exhibit 8-3 provides examples of both strategic and operational issues. Based on channel, division, customer, and unit costs, senior management can make decisions about Strategic Alternatives. Through an ABM study, a manufacturer may find that product delivery through the Internet is half the cost of selling through a dealership. The manufacturer may choose to increase its Internet presence to improve its cost structure. Operationally focused managers can make decisions about how to improve the costs of varied processes. A closer look into the product manufacturing process may reveal that systems costs are causing expenses to rise.

Question	Answer	System
Is there a difference between the cost of an internet sale, direct mail, or sale person originated sale?	Cost By Channel	Strategic
What is the fully loaded cost of producing a unit?	Unit Cost	Strategic
How does the cost structure on a divisional level compare?	Division Cost	Strategic
Are some customers more expensive to do business with than others?	Customer Cost	Strategic
What part of the process are my costs increasing?	Cost by Task	Operational
What is the true cost of training on a new system?	Fully Loaded Training Cost	Operational
Are my process costs changing over time?	Cost of Process	Operational

Exhibit 8-3. ABM: strategic vs. operational issues.

The list in the exhibit is designed to eliminate similar questions, reduce complexity, and limit the level of time and effort for the development. The final matrix balances a wish list with a level of complexity. This will be the end result for the initial iteration of the model. Additional metrics concerning specific strategies or operational issues can be added in later versions. The level of granularity can be to target specific operational processes where there may be opportunities for improvement. As the model is refined, changes must be guided by a simple value proposition. The benefit of the improvement must exceed the cost of analysis. If a specific task has been identified that has a total cost of $100,000, you would not want to spend $110,000 trying to measure it.

Step 2: Create High-Level Process Maps

The next step is to understand the general flow of your processes by mapping your operation. High-level process maps are graphic descriptions of what a company does. These maps are also referred to as value chains. Process maps should include no more than five core processes. Within the core processes, five activities, which are more detailed processes, should be identified (Exhibit 8-4).

An analysis of a detailed process is depicted in Exhibit 8-5.

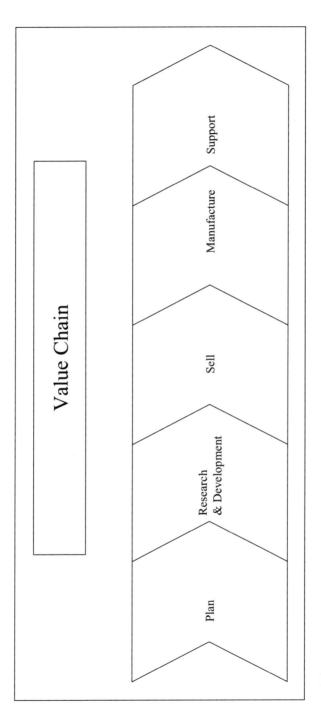

Value Chain

Plan → Research & Development → Sell → Manufacture → Support

Exhibit 8-4. Value chain.

Activity	Financial Value
Strategic Planning	$300,000
Select Target Products	$500,000
Create Prototype Products	$700,000
Test Products	$400,000
Select Products for Launch	$800,000
Administrative Support	$200,000
IT Support	$50,000
Finance Support	$50,000
HR Support	$25,000
Total	$3,025,000

Exhibit 8-5. Analysis of research and development.

This step adds value for two reasons. First, operational redundancies are identified that may lead to the development of shared functions. Shared utilities are departments that are created for common activities throughout the organization, such as HR, purchasing, and finance. For example, divisions may need to purchase technology equipment. Some combination of this function on a company-wide basis may increase economies of scale. If all divisions buy PCs, the cost per PC might be improved by ordering larger quantities.

This will give you an understanding of how your processes fit together and how the connection between business-sustaining functions interrelate with the line functions. For many managers, this will provide an initial insight into day-to-day operations. The important aspect of this step is to understand at a directional level how the processes fit together so that the appropriate resource flow is determined. Many organizations have extremely detailed maps and procedures concerning their processes. These documents can serve as a starting point to derive activity-based maps. Activity-based maps are comprehensive enough to capture the entire activity as well as organizational breadth. Too much detail will increase the time it takes to get results and will not be valuable at the management level. You may choose to increase the level of detail to unearth potential processes after the costing has been completed.

The mapping must be comprehensive of all line and business-sustaining activities. Line activities involve any process or activity that directly contributes to the creation of your product or service. Business-sustaining functions are those that support line functions such as information technology, human resources, and finance.

Step 3: Develop an Activity Dictionary

An activity dictionary is a document that explains your processes in terms of activities and tasks. The

purpose of an activity dictionary is to create a repository for costs in an activity form.

An activity may be comprised of numerous tasks.
Within the recruiting activity you would find the following tasks:

- Placing advertisement
- Contacting and discussing opening with head-
  hunter
- Receiving phone calls from applicants
- Receiving phone calls from headhunters
- Scheduling interviews
- Interviewing candidates
- Selecting candidates
- Notifying candidates

Activity dictionaries are created through interviews with management. As mentioned above, the
amount of detail is dependent on the complexity of
the organization and the strategic/operational results
to be gleaned from the study. The activities and tasks
described in the dictionary should capture 95 percent
of what employees do on a day-to-day basis. Creating
a dictionary is no longer a large undertaking. Standard dictionaries are available for most business
through the International Benchmarking Clearing
House. The standard format can be modified to fit

your specific operation. This exercise is valuable because it gives senior management a view of the business processes. Many times there is a disparity between what happens to get the job done and the executive team's perceptions of day-to-day activities and tasks.

Step 4: Map Costs into Activities

Drivers need to be selected to map costs into activities. Drivers fall into three categories: events, time, and variable rate.

❐ *Events.* Event drivers are simple to use and easy to understand. They are used effectively when events have homogeneous cost characteristics. That is, they require the level of effort from the same type of employees or resource. If events are specialized in nature, then time or variable rate drivers are recommended. Building a car is an example of an event that will trigger costs. Each car requires labor, parts, and the use of facilities, information systems, and electricity. It makes sense that as the number of cars manufactured increases, costs will increase as well. Hypothetically, each automobile may consume three dollars in systems costs. If 100,000 automobiles are built, then $300,000 of information systems costs would be driven into the manufacturing activity.

❏ *Time.* If an electrician spends ten hours at twenty dollars per hour on production line repairs, and then his time at his labor rate is driven into the manufacturing activity ($200), repairs may range from five to thirty hours in duration. A time driver is a better choice because the cost of a repair varies from $100 to $600. The underlying assumption here is that the labor rate for an electrician is in a tight range.

❏ *Variable Rate.* Suppose that an electrical production line repair requires staff with variable experience and labor rates, say from twenty dollars to fifty dollars per hour. The architect of the model would need drivers that would allow for differing labor rates. This type of driver may also apply to different types of assets. Suppose that you were performing an ABM study in a printing company. Different printing presses would have different usage rates based on the age of the press, the size of the paper it was printing, and the number of colors the press was capable of producing.

Step 5: Create Cost Attributes

The beauty of ABM is that it allows you to see your business in numerous ways. Cost attributes are created to capture information to create these views. For example, an attribute can create an analysis of costs driven by separate information technology systems. Attributes are used to make a distinction between fixed and variable costs. A high fixed cost component of an activity indicates that activities would not benefit from reengineering.

Understanding the cost of using and maintaining a system gives you the data to perform an upgrade analysis. One of the benefits of software operation is reduction in operating time.

Step 6: Drive Costs into Strategic Elements

This phase will deliver the strategic intelligence of the ABM initiative. Normally, strategic costing unearths counterintuitive results. Costs are driven into products, customers, channels, and divisions based on the drivers and attributes established in the prior phases of the ABM methodology. The major criticism of ABM is that the entire process is arbitrary and based on subjective rules—the driver selection and consumption. Traditional cost accounting would make allocations based on sales or number of employees, for example. The technique is subjective, but costs do not necessarily link to the metrics used by traditional methods. Doing a product costing for a company may show that its products have a wide range of operating profit margins, say from 53 percent to −7 percent. This differs vastly from a gross profit range of 55 percent to 67 percent. Product number three is a newer product that has required more organizational support because of the staff-up phase, both for line and information technology functions. This information is critical in making decisions about the development of new products in terms of new costs and the additional capacity required for a successful launch.

Strengths of ABM

Here are some of the advantages of ABM:

- ❏ It identifies activities that do not add value. By attaching a monetary value to a process, you are able to assess activities from a monetary perspective. This can tell you if Strategic Alternatives are directed at the right activities.

- ❏ It provides insight into cost by unit of measurement (customer, channel, unit of production). Customers and channels do not have the same resource consumption profile. ABM will tell you if the Strategic Alternative is being directed at the right aspects of your business.

- ❏ By using ABM, you can get a better understanding of resource consumption and allocation. This technique will show you the true cost of a Strategic Alternative by creating a more comprehensive picture of its cost.

Weaknesses of ABM

Here are some of the weaknesses of ABM:

❏ It may create confusion over unit costs in the short run. Once costs are fully loaded into products, activities, and channels, executives may make knee-jerk decisions about abandoning initiatives because of their high cost. It is important to understand the trends in cost and profit before taking action.

❏ This method does not take into account non-financial measurements. It is important to be cost- and profit-conscious, but not at the expense of quality and service. Driving your costs to zero is a going-out-of-business strategy.

Using ABM to Make Strategic Decisions

Costs by product, channel, division, and unit provide a clear picture of the monetary value of these dimensions to your business. These costs are valuable metrics for evaluating Strategic Alternatives and developing scorecards for performance. They can be used to compare the baseline to projected costs of an SA. More focused data on the cost structure and the potential changes that may occur with new initiatives makes you a better decision maker. A more realistic view of the costs associated with product launches may be the deciding data point between a joint venture and de novo entry. The de novo cost may be significantly higher after general and administrative costs are driven into the launch assessment. You also have the ability to measure the results of the implemented decision against your initial baseline for a clearer picture of the performance of the Strategic Alternatives. You can evaluate the performance of the SA against the alternative selected.

Conclusion

To summarize, ABM is a method of looking at your cost structure based on how you do things and not what you spend money on. It differs from traditional accounting because it expresses the cost structure based on your processes and provides a look at the "true" costs of doing business. This method is especially useful when considering reengineering and technology initiatives that involve efficiency-driven value propositions such as cost reduction.

Note

1. Robin Copper and Regine Slagmulder, "Activity-Based Costing Management System Architecture," *Strategic Finance*, October 1999, vol. 81, p. 4.

PART 4

The Valuation Filter

CHAPTER 9

Regression Analysis

An Overview of Regression Analysis

AT ITS MOST BASIC LEVEL, regression analysis is a statistical technique for developing an equation that describes the relationship between two or more variables.[1] This equation generally takes the form of:

$$Y = a + b_1 x_2 + b_2 x_2 + \ldots b_n x_n.$$

The following variables are represented in the equation:

Y equals the dependent variable.

x_n equals the independent variables; the parameters used to predict y.

a equals the value of y when all independent variables are zero.

b_1 equals the regression coefficient that indicates the impact that the independent variables have on the dependent variable.

One variable, the dependent variable, is the variable that you are trying to understand. The dependent variable is the answer. The other variable(s), the independent or explanatory variables, are the factors you feel affect the (dependent) variable or the answer. Let's say a national general merchandise retailer may think that there is a direct relationship between sales and advertising expenditure; more specifically, that an increase in advertising expenditure will result in an increase in total sales. This is based on the rationale that increased advertising will produce greater brand awareness, leading to larger demand for the company's product. In this example, sales are dependent (what you are solving for)—at least to some degree—upon advertising expenditures.

Why Use Regression Analysis?

There are numerous reasons that you might want to use this technique. In general, these reasons fall into one of two categories:

1. *Focus on Drivers.* Regression analysis can be used to identify the "levers" (or explanatory variables) that can most effectively influence or control the value of the dependent variable. Looking again at the national merchandise retailer example, regression analysis shows that advertising expenditures are indeed strongly related to total sales. The firm can then view advertising as one "lever" that can be used to influence or control the value of total sales.

2. *Predicting the Value of a Variable.* Regression analysis can also be used to estimate the future value of a variable. The equation that defines the relationships between the dependent and independent variables can be used in a predictive manner by first replacing explanatory variables with predicted values, then solving the equation to arrive at a predicted value for the dependent variable. To illustrate with the retail example, the analyst may be responsible for creating a five-year strategic plan for the company. This activity requires projecting cash flows for that period of time. If budgetary constraints will reduce advertising expenditures, the analyst can use the regression analysis equation to quantify the future impact on total sales. This function of regression analysis is of great value because of its ability to introduce scientific methods into the forecasting process. In addition, these techniques can be deployed in the economic filter to understand market demand, as

well as in the operational filter as future impacts of financial performance drivers on return on ROA. The basic equations for market demand and the DuPont method can serve as the basic regression equation.

We will focus primarily on exploring regression analysis as a predictive tool and discover its utility and application in the context of the Step-Wise Approach to Value (SWAV).

Types of Regression Analysis

There are two main types of regression analysis techniques that can be applied, depending primarily upon the complexity of the relationships being analyzed: 1) simple linear regression and 2) multiple linear regression. Linear regression analysis, also known as simple linear regression, is applying regression techniques to analyze the relationship between a dependent variable and only one independent or explanatory variable. Multiple regression analysis uses the same fundamental statistical method, but analyzes situations where more than one explanatory variable is thought to be predictive of the dependent variable. Although there are other regression techniques that can be applied in more complex instances, the focus of this book is to provide an introduction to basic statistical tools. Therefore, our discussion will be limited to simple linear regression—the most basic form of regression analysis.

The Regression Analysis Process

At a general level, the three steps in the regression process are:

1. *Develop an equation.* The first step is to identify the question that needs to be answered, and determine the variables that are likely to provide the answer. For example, if the problem is to forecast market demand, you may want to consider variables such as pricing and production.

2. *Collect the data.* The next step is to gather data for the dependent and independent variables in the regression model. In general, analyzing more data will yield more significant results. Therefore, it is common to collect data covering a prolonged time period. Depending upon the variables being analyzed, the data may be retrieved internally, such as from company databases, or externally, such as from public or private sector research organizations.

3. *Conduct and interpret the analysis.* The next step is to input the data into a regression analysis tool

such as Minitab, SPSS, SAS, or Microsoft Excel, depending upon the complexity of the regression analysis. Each software package requires its own method for entering regression model data.

Interpreting Regression Analysis Results

While regression analysis serves as a powerful tool in addressing a wide variety of business issues, it is critical to understand the limits of regression analysis in order to interpret findings most accurately. One of the most common misunderstandings in regression analysis is the assumption that a strong relationship between a dependent variable and an explanatory variable means that the explanatory variable causes changes in the dependent variable. However, this is not always true. It is possible that the reverse is true; that the dependent variable causes changes in the explanatory variable. Linear regression calculations pay no attention to the direction of the relationship.

Another common occurrence is the relationship of unforeseen variables to what is being analyzed. It is possible that the explanatory variable is not a factor in the determination of the dependent variable. For example, one might think that, in a manufacturing environment, an increase in inventory levels will result in a direct increase in labor costs, perhaps based on the assumption that higher inventory levels require additional labor to manage. However, it is important to understand that an increase in overall production can have a direct and simultaneous causal effect on both inventory levels and labor costs. Achieving higher production levels requires additional production capacity (labor) and results in a higher level of inventory as goods await distribution.

Applying Regression Analysis: A Case Example

To demonstrate the utility of regression analysis, we will apply a simple linear regression technique to a hypothetical situation. Auto, Inc., a fictional automobile manufacturer, is interested in estimating the value derived from a proposed Strategic Alternative (SA). The SA, posed by the CEO of the company, is to acquire an elite, high-end auto company where the average retail price of a car is $80,000. As part of this task, the acquisition team develops a three-year market analysis to determine if adequate market demand exists for luxury automobiles. The team chooses to use the predictive power of regression analysis to help make these projections.

Step 1: Develop an Equation

The first step in this process is to understand what drives total market demand for elite, high-end luxury automobiles. After analyzing the industry, the group hypothesizes that gross domestic product, or GDP, is a key predictor of market demand for these automobiles. In this situation there is only one variable with a substantial relationship to total market demand for luxury vehicles. A simple linear regression analysis is used, represented by the equation:

$$Y = a + bx.$$

In the equation, the variables represent the following:

Y equals unit demand for elite, high-end luxury automobiles.

x equals gross domestic product.

a equals the variance in demand not explained by GDP.

b equals the regression coefficient indicating the relationship between GDP and unit demand, or

$$\text{Unit demand} = \text{demand variance} + \text{regression coefficient (GDP)}.$$

This equation expresses that GDP is a key predictor for the market demand for elite, high-end luxury automobiles. With this hypothesis formalized, the company can now gather data for the analysis.

Step 2: Collect the Data

Now that Auto, Inc., has decided to analyze the relationship between GDP and unit demand for these automobiles, the company team can collect the data that will reveal the relationships between those variables. To gather historical GDP data, the team turns to online databases located on the Federal Reserve Board website.[2] To gather data on new vehicle sales for elite, high-end luxury cars, it uses the Bureau of Labor Statistics' online databases on new vehicle car sales.[3] Having consulted these research sources, the following data is gathered in Exhibit 9-1.

While this example analyzes ten years of data, modern statistical software allows for a much more extensive analysis of time-series data. As a rule of thumb, a more complex analysis requires more data to achieve the same level of certainty around the relationships between them.

Step 3: Conduct and Interpret the Analysis

Because popular statistical software such as SPSS, SAS, and Minitab are often expensive, they decide to

Historical New Car Sales (Unit Demand) and GDP Data		
Year	Demand[1] (000's units sold)	GDP[2] (billions of dollars)
1991	2294	5927.9
1992	2706	6221.7
1993	2947	6560.9
1994	2637	6948.8
1995	2619	7322.6
1996	2770	7700.1
1997	2734	8182.8
1998	3393	8636.3
1999	3652	9115.4
2000	3377	9571.9

Exhibit 9-1. The GDP data for Auto, Inc.

use the data analysis function, under the tools menu
item, in the Microsoft Excel application.

When a regression analysis of this data is run in
Excel, the result in a correlation coefficient (the "b"
variable in the equation above) is .60. This coefficient
means that 60 percent of the changes in unit demand
for luxury automobiles can be explained by changes
in the gross domestic product. Because the number is
positive, the changes in each variable are direction-
ally consistent. That is to say that when GDP increases, so do the sales of luxury automobiles. This

number confirms to the team at Auto, Inc., that GDP is a valid predictor of luxury auto sales. With this confirmation, the team can now finish the forecasting process.

The regression analysis the team just performed on the unit demand and GDP data established an equation that describes the relationship between the two variables. This equation can be used to predict the unit demand for luxury cars based on different levels of GDP. Unit demand is the dependent variable, and the GDP is the independent variable in the equation. While this can be done manually, as with most statistical analyses, by "plugging in" predicted GDP values and solving this equation for the unit demand, it can also be done with the forecast function in Excel. This function uses regression analysis to forecast values for a given set of data. However, before the team can forecast unit demand for luxury autos over the next three-year period, the team will have to provide Excel estimates for GDP. Fortunately, the government provides GDP predictions in its historical databases. The team can simply extend the table that was originally created in Excel to include estimated GDP for the years 2001, 2002, and 2003. The forecast function can then be used to calculate predicted unit demand levels in those years. The outcome (illustrated in Exhibit 9-2) would resemble the following:

The output of the analysis in Exhibit 9-2 shows

Unit Demand Predicted from Estimated GDP (2001–2003)		
Year	Demand ('000s units sold)	GDP (billions of dollars)
1991	2294	5927.9
1992	2706	6221.7
1993	2947	6560.9
1994	2637	6948.8
1995	2619	7322.6
1996	2770	7700.1
1997	2734	8182.8
1998	3393	8636.3
1999	3652	9115.4
2000	3377	9571.9
2001	3604	10,041.3
2002	3736	10,502.4
2003	3873	10,982.8

Forecast for Unit Demand { (2001, 2002, 2003)

Exhibit 9-2. Unit demand predicted from estimated GDP (2001 to 2003) for Auto, Inc.

that total unit demand for luxury cars, or number of cars sold, is predicted to reach 3,873 in the year 2003, provided that the GDP reaches its projected level of almost $11 trillion. Assuming an average price of $80,000 per car, the total market demand for elite, high-end luxury cars in 2003 is predicted to be $309,840,000:

$$\text{Total Market Demand} = \text{Price} \times \text{Quantity Demanded}$$
$$= \$80{,}000 \times 3{,}873$$
$$= \$309{,}840{,}000.$$

Of course, the team realizes that Auto, Inc., does not own the market for elite, high-end luxury cars. There-fore, it must take this fact into consideration when attempting to predict the company's realistic market opportunity. Assuming Auto, Inc.'s market share will hover around 30 percent in 2003, the company would have a realistic market opportunity of $93 million:

$$\text{Market Opportunity} = \text{Total Market Demand} \times$$
$$\text{Market Share}$$
$$= \$309{,}840{,}000 \times 30\%$$
$$= \$92{,}952{,}000.$$

The team has now completed its task of predicting total market demand, and the resulting market oppor-tunity, for the Strategic Alternative proposed by the CEO of the company. However, its work does not stop there. To fully evaluate the proposed SA, the team will have to consider the costs of the Strategic Alter-native by building similar predictions. By following a similar process, it can also apply regression analysis techniques to help predict other variables such as the cost of raw materials, labor, and other factors.

Regression-Based Forecasting Using the DuPont Model

The DuPont Model can be used to forecast future changes in ROA using the regression equation, which can be written as follows:

$$ROE = a + b_1ROS + b_2SA + b_3AE.$$

The variables represented in the equation are:

CFM equals cash flow margin.

AT equals asset turnover.

Using historical data, the regression equation can develop regression coefficients to quantify the impact of cash flow margin and asset turnover. This analysis can provide insights on how the independent variables can change ROA and the lagging effects of changes in the business, such as fluctuations in cash flow margin. There may be cyclical patterns in margins based on industry behaviors or economic trends that are not accounted for in the DuPont equation. These fluctuations provide insight into whether a Strategic Alternative can achieve changes in the drivers of financial performance. They are algebraically depicted in the "*a*" term of the equation.

Conclusion

Regression analysis is a useful tool in understanding the relationship of factors that affect SAs. It can be used in the economic filter as a way to estimate market demand as well as in the operational filter to understand how cyclical business patterns may impact drivers of financial performance. The strength of regression is in its predictive power. On the other hand, the technique can deliver suboptimal results when dependent variables are interrelated and are not chosen correctly.

Notes

1. Terry E. Dielman, *Applied Regression Analysis for Business and Economics* (PWS-Kent, 1991).
2. The figures under the column headed "Demand" (Exhibit 9-1) represent new vehicle purchases by the top 20 percent, according to household income, of the consumers in the United States. This information was found on the Federal Reserve Board website.
3. The figures under the column headed "GDP" (Exhibit 9-1) represent the total GDP output of the United States. This information was found on the Bureau of Labor Statistics website.

CHAPTER 10

Components of Value

IN THE PREVIOUS SECTION, we discussed statistical methods that are used to understand relationships
that influence assessment of Strategic Alternatives
(SAs). In this chapter, we will begin to lay the foundation for the valuation filter—a quantitative analysis of
the value derived from SAs. In Chapter 1, we presented the following rendering of intrinsic value:

$$\text{Value} = \frac{\text{Sum of Future Cash Flows}}{\text{Adjustment of Time and Risk}}$$

Here we discuss intrinsic value in a more formal sense. Our purpose is to understand the components of intrinsic value. The mathematical formula for intrinsic value is:

$$NPV = \frac{CF}{(1 + r)^t}$$

The formula's variables are represented as follows:

NPV equals net present value, or the sum of all the cash flows generated by a strategic alterative.

CF equals cash flow for a single period of time, normally a year.

r equals the discount rate or the adjustment for risk.

t equals the time frame in which a cash flow occurs.

While there are many analytical models that can be used to estimate the future value created from a Strategic Alternative, the four fundamental elements that form the foundation of these models are: 1) cash flow, 2) risk, 3) discount rate, and 4) time. It is critical to understand each of these elements in order to carry out a meaningful analysis of shareholder value.

Cash Flow

Simply put, cash flow is an estimate of the cash inflows less the cash outflows that are generated by a Strategic Alternative in a specific period of time.

Cash in
Less
<u>Cash out</u>
Cash flow

It is important to include only cash flows associated with a Strategic Alternative in the analysis. At a high level, cash flows can be classified into three categories: 1) benefits, 2) costs, and, 3) noncash items.

Definition	Source
Cash in	Benefits
Less	Less
<u>Cash out</u>	<u>Costs</u>
Plus	Plus

Noncash items	Depreciation, amortization, and depletion
Cash flow	Cash flow

Benefits

Benefits are derived from monetizing the value propositions we discussed in Chapter 1. The three value propositions are:

1. Revenue increase/maintenance (RIM)

2. Competitive repositioning

3. Efficiency

Examples of how benefits can be identified are in Exhibit 10-1.

Costs

Costs are all cash outflows associated with a strategic initiative that are directly related to the strategic initiative. At a high level, costs can be considered payment for the resources required to implement and sustain the strategic initiative. As an example, acquisitions often require technology systems integration between two companies to eliminate redundancies

SA	Value Proposition	Benefit Stream
M&A	Revenue Increase	Projected revenue from acquisition
Technology	Revenue Maintenance	Revenue lost to competitors if SA not implemented
Technology	Competitive repositioning (Increase in market share)	Increase in market share and subsequent lift in revenue from implementation of point-of-sale technology
Reengineering	Efficiency	Cost savings from elimination of activities

Exhibit 10-1. How benefits can be identified.

and ensure consistent business operation. This can require outside expertise in systems integration, internal labor costs, and perhaps the purchase of additional software and hardware.

Costs can be classified into the following three categories:

1. *Investment Costs.* Investment costs are easy outflows that become assets. These costs appear on a company's balance sheet and typically involve the purchase of:

   ❑ Physical assets—e.g., property and equipment, (For example, a car company that wants to diversify by making golf carts will have to purchase specialized manufacturing machinery.)

   ❑ Working capital—e.g., inventory, accounts receivable, and consumables items. (This can include inventory such as the raw materials, such as sheet metal, that are needed to build the golf carts in the previous example.)

   ❑ Intangible assets—e.g., acquisition of software patents and trademarks. (Using the same example, this can include the purchase of a patent on a superior golf cart design.)

   Investment costs are used to calculate noncash charges such as depreciation and amortization.

2. *Operating Costs.* Operating costs are all costs required to sustain a strategic initiative. To build on our automotive company example, the plant machinery that is specifically for the assembly of golf carts will require ongoing maintenance. This maintenance expense can be attributed directly to this strategic initiative and should be accounted for as an operating cost cash flow.

3. *Termination Costs.* Termination costs are all costs required to either terminate the Strategic Alternative or to transition it from one significant lifecycle stage to the next. Continuing with the auto company diversification example, costs associated with the sale of the company based on the holding period of the company can be considered termination costs.

Noncash Items: Impact of Taxes on Cash Flows

To accurately identify the cash flows generated from an SA, it is important to remember to consider tax implications. Cash flow projections should reflect after-tax values to present a more accurate picture of the ultimate value derived from a Strategic Alternative. This requires the adjustment made in Exhibit 10-2.

Let's illustrate using our supply chain manage-

Benefits
Less: costs
Net benefits
Less: taxes (net benefits $\times$ tax rate)
Plus: noncash charges
Cash flow

Exhibit 10-2. Cost-benefit analysis.

ment system implementation (see Exhibit 10-3). The annual cash flow derived from the system is $9 million. There are two methods of calculated tax impact and hence the cash flow. Let's use the method above that assumes the noncash charges are included in the initial tax estimate. Assume that total expenses are $17 million, where $12 million is operating costs plus $5 million in noncash charges. Noncash charges were spread over six years (investment costs of $30 million divided by six). You would simply add the noncash charges that are already included in the cost.

If noncash charges are not included in costs, the calculation involves adding the product of noncash charges to the difference between benefits less costs and taxes ($6 million times a tax rate of 32 percent).

Risk Analysis

Risk analysis assures that the management team has a complete understanding of an SA. A risk is defined as

Noncash Charge Included in Costs	(rounded to the nearest million)
Benefits: Saving on inventory handling	$23
Less: Costs (operating cost plus reengineering)	$17
Net benefits	$6
Less: taxes (net benefits × tax rate)*	$2
Plus: noncash charges	$5
Cash flow	$9

Noncash charges included in costs	
Benefits: saving on inventory handling	$23
Less: costs (operating cost plus reengineering)	$12
Net benefits	$11
Less: taxes (net benefits × tax rate)*	$4
Add: noncash charges × tax rate	$2
Cash flow	$9

*Tax rate is 32 percent.

Exhibit 10-3. Cash flow.

an issue that may have a negative impact on the intrinsic value generated from a Strategic Alternative. This means identifying issues that have an effect on intrinsic value. The analysis entails identifying specific risks and ways to mitigate them. A risk template is the outcome of this analysis. The risk template gives you an overall risk assessment of a Strategic Alternative. This assessment is used to make quantitative adjustments in value. The risk analysis will provide the necessary information to adjust for risk through the cost of capital and some premium above the cost of capital if necessary. We will discuss fundamental risks that are prevalent with all strategic alternatives here. Risks can be put in the following categories:

- Recognition of benefits
- Timing
- Cost overruns

Recognition of Benefits

Recognition risk is the inability to realize the projected benefits established prior to implementation. It is normally caused by unrealistic goal setting and is very common among mergers and acquisitions activity. Suppose a company is considering an acquisition for purposes of revenue enhancement. The projection is to increase revenues by 10 percent. Anything that may impede this revenue increase can be considered a risk (such as poor economic conditions and loss of customers). Many of these factors cannot be controlled by management. In fact, management can be its own worst enemy by creating recognition risks. To sell the concept to shareholders, aggressive and unachievable goals may be set.

Timing

Time is an issue in all aspects of business. Speed can be the difference between success and failure. Compression of time can cause failure, affect accuracy and quality, and drain morale. Timing risk can be tied to time to completion, costs, and benefits of an initiative. Delay in time drives reduction in value (such as slower integration of operations) and lowers cost synergies. Let's look at some of the timing risks associated with the revenue enhancement merger discussed in the previous example.

- ❑ Completion—Delays in closing the transaction may hinder a company's ability to compete.

- ❑ Benefits—The buying company would realize revenues later than expected.

- ❑ Costs—Integration costs may be incurred earlier than expected.

Cost Overruns

The risk of underestimating costs associated with implementation is always high. Risk tends to decline with experience. Companies that have established a core competency in executing specific SAs experience greater success in managing expenses of initiatives. Higher than expected integration costs would lead to lower cash flows. Cost overruns may also appear because of poor anticipation of all the expenses required to implement an SA.

Cost of Capital—Adjustment for Risk

Another major component required to estimate the intrinsic value is the cost of capital. As mentioned, the cost of capital is used as a benchmark in adjustment for risk. The cost of capital is generally considered an opportunity cost because it represents the return forgone by investing in the Strategic Alternative rather than in other investments that yield a return.[1] In the world of finance, the term capital is often used in several ways. For example, capital assets, sometimes called fixed assets, refer to the land, buildings, machinery, and equipment used in the operation of the business. However, in computing the cost of capital we will consider two types of capital: debt and equity. To calculate the total cost of capital, it is necessary to compute the combined cost of debt and equity capital. This is commonly referred to as the weighted average cost of capital, or WACC. Let's walk through how to calculate the cost of debt, the cost of equity, and ultimately the weighted average cost of capital.

Cost of Debt

Debt capital is the investment in a company by creditors for the purpose of earning interest. Total debt is simply the total of all interest-bearing debt, or total liabilities less the liabilities on which interest is not paid. Liabilities, such as accounts payable and accrued liabilities, do not earn interest and are not considered in the calculation. The two inputs we will use to arrive at the total amount of debt capital and the effective (after-tax) interest rate. Calculation of the effective interest rate will be shown below.

There are several ways to obtain the interest rate on debt capital. One of the simplest ways is to find the interest rate stated in the footnotes to the financial statements of a company. An alternative is to review The Value Line Investment Survey® or similar research reports. Value Line® reports the financial strength of a company in a box at the lower right corner of the company's report. Financial strength is given an alphabetic ranking from A + +, the strongest ranking, to C, which is the weakest. The interest rates at which a company can borrow vary according to financial strength. Another method is to check with the rating agencies that make these assessments. The corresponding interest rates for these ratings are found in *The Wall Street Journal.*

To calculate the effective interest rate we must

first have the income tax rate. This also may be found in the Value Line Reports®. The effective interest rate is calculated as follows:

$$[\text{Incremental interest rate}] \times (1 - \text{Tax Rate}) =$$
$$[\text{Effective Interest Rate}]$$

Assume a company has an A + + rating. Its interest rate would then be 6.0 percent. With an income tax rate of 32 percent, the effective interest rate would be calculated as follows:

6. $0 \times (1 - .32) = 4.1\%$.

This rate represents the cost of the company's cost of debt capital and can now be combined with the company's cost of equity capital to arrive at the total cost of capital.

Cost of Equity Capital

Many managers and accountants challenge the concept of the cost of capital because it involves some subjectivity in the selection of inputs. However, investors expect to be compensated for taking risk. Traditional accounting does not deal with this issue. The cost of equity is derived from the capital asset pricing

model (CAPM), which can be calculated using the following formula:

$$\text{Cost of Equity (Ke)} = \text{Risk Free Rate} +$$
$$\text{Equity Risk Premium}$$
$$\text{Or}$$
$$Ke = Rf + \beta\,(Rm{-}Rf)$$

The values in the formula are represented as follows:

❑ R_f is the risk-free rate for U.S. treasury bonds.
The rate for U.S. treasury long bonds can be
found daily in *The Wall Street Journal, USA
Today*, or many other leading newspapers
throughout the world.

❑ Rm is the expected rate of return provided by
the stock market as a whole. The figure is usually the rate of return for a broad market basket
of stocks, such as those listed on the Standard
and Poor 500.

❑ ß is the beta coefficient, or risk factor. The risk
factor is a multiplier that reflects the risk of the
Strategic Alternative that is being analyzed
versus the broader risk of alternative investments.

Beta

Most investors want to be compensated for taking on more risk. The beta coefficient was conceived to deal with this issue. It measures the risk associated with the common stock of a given company relative to the stock market as a whole. Beta measures the relative volatility of a company's stock to the price movements in the market. Therefore, a stock's beta measures its contribution to the overall riskiness of a portfolio or a group of stocks. So theoretically, beta is a correct measure of riskiness.

$\beta > 1$ = greater volatility than the market
$\beta < 1$ = lower volatility than the market

If stocks with greater-than-average betas ($\beta > 1$) are added to a portfolio, the riskiness of the portfolio increases. Conversely, if stocks with below-average betas ($\beta < 1$) are added, the portfolio's overall risk level will decrease. Therefore, a beta of one means that the common stock of the company in question moves exactly with the market as a whole. If the company, or strategic project, is an "average" risk, use a beta factor of one.

The beta of a listed corporation can also be found in a company's Value Line® report. If beta is not listed, risk becomes a matter of judgment.

Assume a company has a beta of 1.2. The thirty-year Treasury Bond (Rf) carries interest at 5 percent and the market return (Rm) is 10 percent.

$Ke = Rf + \beta(Rm{-}Rf)$

$5\% + 1.2\,(10\%{-}5\%) = 11.0\%$

Weighted Average Cost of Capital

Now that we have calculated the cost of debt and the cost of equity, we find a single rate that reflects the cost of capital. We can do this by computing the weighted cost of capital. The weighted average is computed by first determining the percentage of total capital that is comprised of debt and the percentage that is comprised of equity. The percentages are available in Value Line® reports, in the section noted as "Capital Structure."

The percent of debt is multiplied by the effective (after-tax) interest rate. The percent of equity is multiplied by the rate representing the cost of equity. They are then added together to find the rate representing the cost of capital.

Assume that our company has debt capital representing 40 percent of invested capital, with the remaining representing equity capital. The cost of capital rate is:

1. Debt Capital $= 40\% \times 4.1\% = 1.6\%$
2. Equity Capital $= 60\% \times 11.00\% = +6.6\,\%$
3. Weighted Average Cost of Capital $= 8.2\%$

Accounting for Risk in
Shareholder Value Analysis

The cost of capital creates a benchmark for risk. Many firms use the cost of capital as a baseline and add a risk premium above the cost of capital to account for the risks discussed above. The cost of capital then becomes the minimum discount rate used for capital investments. The cost of capital would be used to discount more conservative investments such as real estate. More speculative projects such as implementation of state-of-the-art technology would command a discount rate of 50 percent or a return analogous to that of a venture capital fund.

Another method of accounting for risk is to use simulation techniques, which will be discussed in Chapter 11.

Conclusion

In this chapter, we explored concepts that are fundamental to an analysis of shareholder value. First, we discussed how to create a cash flow model by accounting for the benefits and costs of a Strategic Alternative. We then learned about primary sources of risk, how they impact our shareholder value analysis, and ways to mitigate them. Finally, we explored the concept of cost of capital. We learned that the total cost of capital, also known as the weighted average cost of capital, consists of the cost of equity and the cost of debt and that it is used to determine the discount rate—the rate used to convert future cash flows to their present values. In Chapter 11, we will apply these fundamental analytical components to explore alternative methods for estimating the future value created from a Strategic Alternative.

Note

1. Richard A. Brealy and Stewart C. Myers, *Principles of Corporate Finance*, 6th ed. (New York: McGraw Hill, 2000).

Valuation

IN CHAPTER 10, we discussed the components of value. With a strong understanding of these elements and how they affect valuation, we are ready to complete the assessment of the valuation filter in the Step-Wise Approach to Value (SWAV). This involves applying analytical techniques to monetize (put in dollar terms) the value of the Strategic Alternative (SA). Remember that we are calculating intrinsic value, which is an estimate of the value derived from the future cash flows of an SA. Since we are dealing with estimation, the outcome of this filter should not only provide a quantification of value, but an understanding of how good the estimate is. This assessment requires the use of numerous tools depending on the level of uncertainty around the estimate.

Portfolio of Analytical Tools

Broadly speaking, the choice of which analytical tool to apply depends largely on the level of uncertainty inherent in a given Strategic Alternative. The discounted cash flow (DCF) analysis method is a bedrock analytical tool that can be applied to the evaluation of all SAs, and it provides a rather straightforward manner to determine estimated cash flows resulting from a Strategic Alternative. For instance, in assessing a food company acquisition, an analyst will be able to predict market demand for food with a relatively high degree of certainty. However, it will be useful to perform additional analyses under conditions of uncertainty. When analyzing Strategic Alternatives where you are less confident about the results, alternative methods such as financial modeling techniques can be used. In general, these techniques will help you to better understand how changes in the components of value can impact the future value of an SA. For example, this can include situations such as implementing cutting-edge technology where the cash flows are less certain. Financial modeling techniques include such methods as break-even analysis, sensitivity analysis, scenario analysis, and Monte Carlo simulation.

Discounted Cash Flow Analysis (DCF): The Analytical Foundation

Discounted cash flow analysis is a technique used to identify the value of a Strategic Alternative where future cash flows are discounted or converted to their present value. DCF is important in strategic planning because it translates the monetary impact of forward-looking decisions into today's value. We discussed the math for DCF in the last chapter; here we will talk about the process. The following three steps are used to conduct a discounted cash flow analysis:

1. *Calculate the cash flows.* In arriving at the cash flows, the important things to remember are to be realistic and comprehensive. A test of realism is to provide numbers that the most conservative individual on your team will deem reasonable. In order to be comprehensive you need to make sure that you are capturing all the elements of the cash flow. The norm is that the staff will be good about making sure that the entire benefit dimension is accounted for and the cost side is not comprehen-

sive. Remember to include all the investment and operating costs, as discussed in Chapter 10. This is a big issue in the evaluation of technology projects where costs are not fully sized, and initiatives are abandoned because of the high expense to develop and operate systems. As you move through this exercise, try to gain an understanding about the uncertainty of the cash flows. Your judgment on the accuracy of our estimates is input for the next step. Low levels of accuracy do not mean that the analysis is flawed. There are cases where large amounts of data are not available. Say you are evaluating outsourcing all your administrative functions—information technology, accounting, human resources, and purchasing. Let's assume that your company has not outsourced anything in the past and there are a limited number of companies that have done this. This case would be of lower accuracy because of the limited amount of experience that you can draw on. You may want to use financial modeling techniques to gain an additional understanding of the value impact.

2. *Select a discount rate.* As discussed in the prior chapter, the discount rate is the rate used to adjust the future cash flows for risk. This is the driver of the adjustment for risk. Great care needs to be taken in the selection of this component since it has a large impact on the value of future cash

flows. You will need to compare this case against other Strategic Alternatives to determine its relative risk. This comparison will drive the decision to attach a premium to the cost of capital.

3. *Compute the net present value.* Net present value is simply the sum of all the cash flows. This represents the increase or decrease in value that can be attributed to the Strategic Alternative. If the net present value is positive, then the Strategic Alternative should be implemented. If the net present value is negative, then the Strategic Alternative should be not be pursued at the time of the analysis. Future conditions may change the economics of the alternative.

Applying DCF Analysis

To develop a thorough understanding of how to apply discounted cash flow analysis, we will apply it to a hypothetical situation with a fictional company. A chain of coffee houses, Wide Awake, is considering expanding its network through the Strategic Alternative of acquiring a significant competitor, Caffeine City. Let's apply discounted cash flow analysis to estimate the intrinsic value of this alternative. The first step in the process is to identify all future cash inflows and outflows resulting from the SA.

Step 1: Determine Free Cash Flows

Cash inflows consist of all expected revenues earned from the implementation of a Strategic Alternative. Cash outflows are all costs incurred over the life of the strategic initiative. Cash outflows are divided into investment costs and operating costs. Investment costs are items that become assets or things that a business owns.

In this case, the acquisition price—which is considered our initial investment in this case—is $50 million. The annual free cash flows start at $16 million per year and grow at 10 percent annually. The company will be sold at year five for $75 million. Exhibit 11-1 is a simple time line illustrating the cash flows associated with this Strategic Alternative.

Step 2: Select a Discount Rate

Let's assume that the discount rate, or cost of capital, is 15 percent. To review how to arrive at an appropriate discount rate, please refer to the section on shareholder value analysis in Chapter 10.

Step 3: Compute the Net Present Value

In the final step, we will apply a 15 percent discount rate factor to calculate the present value of the free

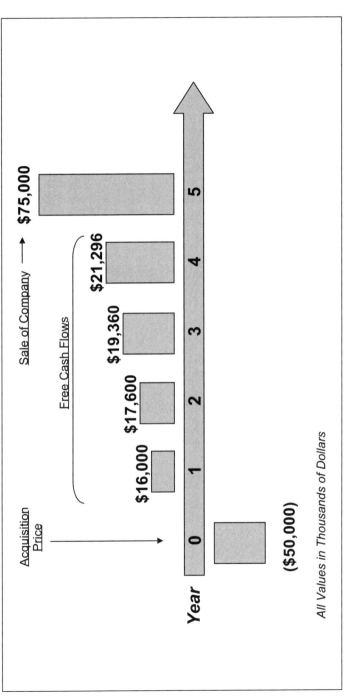

Exhibit 11-1. Projected net cash flows for Caffeine City acquistion, version A.

cash flows in each future time period (Exhibit 11-2). Following this, all cash flows—whether positive or negative—will be summed for all time periods in the analysis to arrive at the net present value (NPV) of the Strategic Alternative in question. .

According to our discounted cash flow analysis, the net present value of the acquisition is approximately $39.4 million. This means that the Strategic Alternative creates intrinsic value and will increase the shareholder value of Wide Awake by $39.4 million.

While this example proves that DCF analysis is a relatively straightforward method for estimating the future value created from a proposed SA, the method is not without its limitations. One of the most significant weaknesses is that the outcome is more substantially influenced by cash flows that occur further out in time, which are much more difficult to predict accurately. Essentially, the net present value hinges most on those cash flows that are harder to predict. In the Wide Awake analysis, the majority of the NPV was generated in year five. It also had the highest adjustment for risk. Additionally, selection of the discount rate is a highly subjective, unscientific process involving consideration of multiple variables. How much does the discount rate affect intrinsic value? Let's look at the impact of changing the discount rate on intrinsic value. For example, we could reduce the discount rate to 12 percent (Exhibit 11-3).

As further illustrated in Exhibit 11-4, the net

(text continues on page 234)

Year	Cash Flow*	Discount Factor @ (15%)**	Present Value of Cash Flow*
0	($50,000)	1.0000	($50,000)
1	$16,000	0.8696	$13,914
2	$17,600	0.7561	$13,307
3	$19,360	0.6575	$12,729
4	$21,296	0.5718	$12,177
5	$75,000	0.4972	$37,290
NPV			$39,417

*Values in thousands of dollars.

**Discount rate factors can be found in corporate finance books when discount rate and number of time periods is known.

Exhibit 11-2. Computing net present value.

Year	Cash Flow*	Discount Factor @ (12%)**	Present Value of Cash Flow*
0	($50,000)	1.0000	($50,000)
1	$16,000	0.8929	$14,286
2	$17,600	0.7972	$14,031
3	$19,360	0.7118	$13,780
4	$21,296	0.6355	$13,534
5	$75,000	0.5674	$42,555
NPV			$48,186

*Values in thousands of dollars.

**Discount rate factors can be found in corporate finance books when discount rate and number of time periods is known.

Exhibit 11-3. Computing net present value with a reduction in the discount rate.

Year	Varying Discount Rates		Net Increase / (Decrease)
	12%	15%	
1	$14,286	$13,914	$ 372
2	$14,031	$13,307	$ 724
3	$13,780	$12,729	$1,051
4	$13,534	$12,177	$1,357
5	$42,555	$37,290	$5,265
NPV	$48,186	$39,417	$8,769

Exhibit 11-4. Present value of future cash flows.

present value increases by about $9 million with only a 3 percent reduction in discount rate (15 percent to 12 percent). As we can see, the change in the discount rate has a dramatic impact on value, particularly on the cash flows that come later in the time frame of the analysis. The most dramatic jump is in year five, with a $5.3 million dollar increase.

Assessing Value Under Uncertain Conditions

As we have seen, DCF presents a straightforward method for calculating the intrinsic value of an SA under conditions where future inputs or outputs are relatively certain, such as in the example of a food company acquisition mentioned earlier in this chapter. In these situations, the information used is more or less readily available at the time of the analysis and is not expected to vary significantly. However, under conditions where information used to predict cash flows is highly variable, financial modeling techniques can be used to get a better understanding of the range of outcomes. The appropriate method to be used depends on the complexity of the assessment.

Financial Modeling Techniques

While uncertainty is inherent in planning any strategic undertaking, it is possible to apply analytical techniques that acknowledge the presence of uncertainty and help us to understand its potential economic impact on the overall business strategy. Four proven techniques that are commonly used for this purpose are:

1. Break-even analysis
2. Sensitivity analysis
3. Scenario analysis
4. Simulation analysis

We will now provide an overview of each method and talk about the strengths and weaknesses of each.

Break-Even Analysis

Break-even analysis occurs when the benefits of an SA equal the cost of its operation. Break-even analysis is important because it identifies the value needed to create a self-sustaining initiative. It can be calculated in various ways, examples of which include:

❐ Number of units
❐ Dollar volume processed
❐ Revenues generated
❐ Number of users
❐ Number of FTEs (full-time employees) redeployed

Run Like Crazy, Inc., a retailer of running shoes, is considering selling online. The average pair of running shoes sells for eighty dollars. The fully loaded cost (which includes all costs of sale such as labor, shelf space, etc.) of a pair of shoes (based on an ABM study) is forty-eight dollars per pair. The profit per pair of shoes is thirty-two dollars:

Cost of Manual Process	$80
Cost of Automated Process	−$48
Savings per Transaction	$32

Assume that the cost to operate the online sales system is $8 million. What is the break-even sales volume necessary to justify the system?

Annual Operating Costs	$8,000,000
Savings per Transaction	÷$32
Break-Even Transaction Volume	$250,000

Conducting this simple analysis will help us understand the inherent risk in this project. If you compare current sales volume levels with the calculated break-even point for this system, you can get an idea of the likelihood of reaching break-even transaction levels. If our company had a current sales volume that was less than $250,000, the firm would probably be taking a big risk in implementing the system. The beauty of break-even analysis is that it is simple to understand and relatively easy to perform. On the other hand, it does not provide a range of estimates and assumes that no value is being generated.

Sensitivity Analysis

The purpose of a sensitivity analysis (for the purposes of our work) is to understand how variances in such things as benefits, costs, and other components of value affect intrinsic value. More specifically, a sensitivity analysis will show the change in net present value of an SA, where key inputs vary over a range of values. The benefit of conducting this analysis is that it helps to reveal the variables that have greatest influence over the potential success of the SA.

Drawing upon our earlier example that demonstrated discounted cash flow analysis, we will apply a sensitivity analysis to Wide Awake's acquisition of Caffeine City. The sensitivity analysis can be used to show us what would happen to the NPV of the Strategic Alternative if there were a change in the estimated growth rate of the cash flows generated by the acquisition. Before, we assumed these cash flows would grow at 10 percent annually. However, there is a possibility that market demand for coffee will decline, perhaps due to the effects of a lagging economy on discretionary spending. In this case, it may be reasonable to assume cash flows from the acquisition would grow at a slower rate, perhaps at only 5 percent annually (Exhibit 11-5). Under this condition, our cash flows would be similar to those in Exhibit 11-1.

Now, if we apply the same discount rate—15 percent—to the change in projected cash flows, we arrive

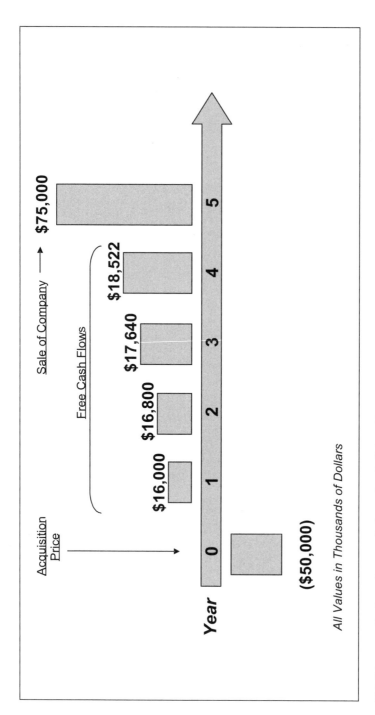

Exhibit 11-5. Projected net cash flows for Caffeine City acquistion, version B.

at the following NPV for the acquisition (Exhibit 11-6).

Exhibit 11-6 shows the net present value of the project, assuming cash flows grow at 5 percent annually, instead of at 10 percent annually. At 5 percent annual growth, the net present value of the SA is $36.1 million, whereas at 10 percent annual growth, the net present value of the project is $39.4 million. The sensitivity analysis shows us that a 5 percent reduction in the growth rate of cash flows generated from the acquisition will result in a decrease of $3.3 million in the estimated value of the project. If the sensitivity is performed for a range of growth rates between 5 percent and 10 percent, the outcome would be a sensitivity analysis, as depicted in Exhibit 11-7.

The sensitivity shows the impact of a change in growth rate on the discounted cash flow for years two to four and the NPV overall. (Recall that the years one and five do not change. The discounted values in year one is $13,914, and year five is fixed at $37,290.) What the analysis shows is the incremental difference in the net present value based on a downward pressure in growth. The decision maker can get a quick understanding of the decline in value throughout the range. So if you feel that a 5 percent drop is too steep, you can see what the impact would be of a more reasonable decline, such as a 3 percent reduction in growth.

The power of sensitivity analysis is that it shows

(text continues on page 242)

Caffeine City Acquistion: Net Present Value @ 5% Annual Growth

Year	Revised Cash Flow*	Discount Factor @ (15%)**	Present Value of Cash Flow*
0	($50,000)	1.0000	($50,000)
1	$16,000	0.8696	$13,914
2	$16,800	0.7561	$12,703
3	$17,640	0.6575	$11,598
4	$18,522	0.5718	$10,591
5	$75,000	0.4972	$37,290
NPV			$36,096

*Values in thousands of dollars.
**Discount rate factors can be found in corporate finance books when discount rate and number of time periods is known.

Exhibit 11-6. Projected net present value for Caffeine City acquisition.

NPV	Growth Rate 5%	6%	7%	8%	9%	10%
2	$12,703	$12,823	$12,944	$13,065	$13,186	$13,307
3	$11,598	$11,820	$12,044	$12,271	$12,499	$12,729
4	$10,591	$10,896	$11,208	$11,525	$11,848	$12,177
NPV	$36,095	$36,744	$37,400	$38,064	$38,737	$39,417

Exhibit 11-7. Caffeine City acquisition growth rate.

the progression of a result against different levels of selected variables. It is a positive exercise because it forces managers to understand key variables driving the success or failure of a project and identifies areas where additional information may be beneficial. This tool also has its limits. One of the drawbacks is that the results can often be considered somewhat ambiguous. When asking different forecasters to provide optimistic and pessimistic projections, it is important to understand that each forecaster may define optimistic and pessimistic differently based on subjective interpretations. Another weakness of sensitivity analysis is that it neglects the fact that variables are often interrelated. For example, an increase in market size is likely associated with higher marketing costs. Given these inherent weaknesses, sensitivity analysis should not be viewed as a complete solution for finding the estimated future value of a Strategic Alternative.

Scenario Analysis

Scenario analysis uses the same fundamental techniques as sensitivity analysis. However, the method attempts to address one of the primary limitations of sensitivity analysis by taking into consideration how certain variables may be interrelated. Instead of altering a single variable independently and observing the change in net present value, you can consider a scenario under which a number of related variables may change, resulting in a collective change in net present value. Using the Wide Awake acquisition of Caffeine City as an illustration, it is logical to assume that the same lagging economy that limits growth in market demand for coffee may also produce lower yields on other investments in the capital markets. This may cause discount rates to decline so the scenario we are analyzing takes into account the potential for slower growth rate in cash flows between 5 percent and 10 percent, and a discount rate of 10 percent instead of 15 percent. Exhibit 11-8 shows the NPV of the acquisition of Caffeine City under these scenarios.

Our scenario analysis shows that if the economy weakened to the point where growth for coffee was slower than predicted, the estimated value of the acquisition could range from $39.4 million to $36.1 million, or a variance of $3.3 million. At the same time, if the SA team thought that this transaction was lower-risk, the value would increase to $54.8 million, based on a 10 percent growth rate.

Despite the fact that scenario analysis attempts to compensate for a key limitation of sensitivity analysis—lack of consideration for the interrelationships between variables—it would be unwise to consider it the end-all solution to estimating future value creation for a Strategic Alternative. The other weakness inherent in sensitivity analysis, the presence of subjectivity, still presents a barrier to more accurate pre-

	Growth Rate					
Year						
	5%	6%	7%	8%	9%	10%
Discount Rate						
10%	$50,903	$51,654	$52,414	$53,183	$53,962	$54,751
11%	$47,658	$48,386	$49,124	$49,871	$50,627	$51,392
12%	$44,562	$45,270	$45,986	$46,711	$47,445	$48,187
13%	$41,608	$42,295	$42,991	$43,695	$44,407	$45,128
14%	$38,788	$39,455	$40,131	$40,814	$41,506	$42,207
15%	$36,095	$36,744	$37,400	$38,064	$38,737	$39,417

Exhibit 11-8. Caffeine City acquisition scenario analysis.

dictions. Additionally, even though a relationship between variables may be obvious, it is impossible to know the exact degree to which each variable relates to the other. However, more sophisticated methods exist that attempt to make these predictions more scientific in nature using probabilistic and statistical methods.

Monte Carlo Simulation

While sensitivity analysis allows you to consider the effect of changing one variable at a time, and scenario analysis evaluates a change in multiple variables, Monte Carlo simulation is an analytical tool used when considering all possible combinations of variables (see Exhibit 11-9). In short, Monte Carlo simulation allows you to analyze multiple variables simultaneously as well as account for the range of possible values within each of those variables. These scenarios are tested through random sampling techniques. To do this, the analysis takes into account the probability associated with all possible outcomes of each variable. Ultimately, the simulation arrives at cash flow estimates that illustrate the full spectrum of possibilities, assuming that original estimations for variable ranges and probabilities are accurate. Using the Caffeine City example further, the steps in the Monte Carlo simulation process are as follows:

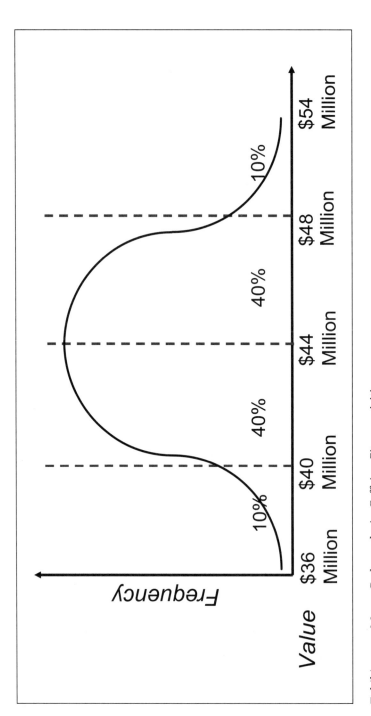

Exhibit 11-9. Monte Carlo analysis, Caffeine City acquisition.

1. *Model the project.* The first step in the process is to create a model of the SA that illustrates the relationships between the project's variables mathematically. Taking market size as one example of a variable, it is important to understand that an off-target estimation for one year requires an adjustment in the estimation for the following year. This can be linked to Caffeine City's cash flows.

2. *Specify probabilities.* The next step in the process is to specify the probability of error in forecasting each of the variables in the model. Using the example of market size again, an analyst may expect the total market size to be 1 million consumers while acknowledging that it may be as low as 500,000 or as high as 1.5 million, depending on macroeconomic factors, for instance. Assuming this range is established with absolute certainty, the remaining step is to assign probabilities to each distinct value within that range.

3. *Simulate cash flows.* The final step is to calculate the estimated cash flows based on the model and probabilities defined previously. In the real world, this would be done with software designed specifically for this purpose.

A Monte Carlo analysis yields a range of values. If we look at an illustration that uses this analysis on

the Caffeine City acquisition (Exhibit 11-9) we might
find that there is a:

❏ 10 percent chance that the value will be between
$36 million and $40 million

❏ 40 percent chance that the value will be between
$41 million and $44 million

❏ 40 percent chance that the value will be between
$45 million and $48 million

❏ 10 percent chance that the value will be between
$49 million and $54 million

The strength of this analysis is that it provides
detail around the variability of the valuation. Just getting one number using a traditional discounted cash
flow does not provide you with a level of confidence
regarding the answer. The weakness is that Monte
Carlo is a highly sophisticated tool that, if misused,
will distort rather than refine the view of the valuation.

Conclusion

In conclusion, this chapter discussed analytical methods in the valuation filter of the Step-Wise Approach
to Value. Several tools—depending on the level of un-

certainty—can be used to estimate future value created from a Strategic Alternative. Discounted cash
flow analysis is an analytical method that can be applied to the evaluation of SAs where future cash flows
can be predicted with relative certainty, primarily because information used to predict cash flows is abun-
dant, highly relevant, and reflects a relatively stable
environment. In situations that involve more uncertainty in the projection of future cash flows, financial
modeling techniques can be used to achieve a more
accurate estimate of future value. The techniques we
learned include break-even analysis, sensitivity analysis, scenario analysis, and Monte Carlo simulation.
They are valuable because they help us understand
the uncertainty inherent in specific variables associated with a Strategic Alternative.

Final Thoughts

I HAVE DESCRIBED a sound analytical framework that is grounded in theory and practice. I could claim my job is done. The truth is, I want you to be successful. This requires me to be realistic about how you should execute what I have discussed. The topics in this section may seem counterintuitive to most of you. One would assume that the techniques discussed in this book would be easily deployed with adequate training in an organization. Most executives think that analytical models are easily embraced by their staff because they are perceived as tools to assist in the decision-making process. Yet, there are a whole set of issues that have nothing to do with the soundness of the tool that need to be addressed for the Step-Wise Approach to Value (SWAV) to be successful. In extreme cases what we have found in our work is that assessment techniques that are vague, illogical, and qualitative are often put in place. They do not link back to value. These methods do not serve the shareholder, but those who are in control of them. As a result, value is destroyed, not enhanced. Consequently, you need to be aware of these issues. They may be present in your organization and can pose significant barriers to success.

We have seen the best analytical tools be dismissed and or misused due to the lack of attention to the dark side of valuation, process issues, and organizational considerations. This not only applies to the SWAV, but to Strategic Alternatives as well. The dark side of valuation deals with the central notion of valuation and measurement. Organizational dynamics focus on the perceptual aspects of the implementation of the SWAV. Process issues are steps that can be taken to increase the probability of success. In this section we will examine each of these issues and then discuss our thoughts on how you can best execute the Step-Wise Approach to Value.

The Dark Side of Valuation

There is a dark side to every conceptual system. The dark side of the SWAV lies in the underlying concept of value and how the framework is perceived by those who use the method. The methods described in the SWAV can be perceived as threatening or even offensive to many individuals in your company. The first problem is with the concept of value itself. Whenever we travel throughout the country to teach a course on the valuation of information technology to upper management, we ask each manager to independently define value and then present the definition to the group. The purpose of the exercise is to demonstrate how diverse the concept of value is and to identify measurement issues. The exercise also helps to create consensus around the notion of intrinsic value and its quantitative attributes. After this discussion the group invariably accepts the notion of intrinsic value with ease. Yet intrinsic value has some blind sides. This measurement of value is monetary in nature—it is appropriate for capitalistic systems. There may be other views of value and hence other metrics to assess them. For example, many development banks (such as the World Bank) measure value by other means. They look at increased value by monitoring infant mortality, distribution of income, and the percentage of individuals suffering from poverty. However, we have constructed the SWAV framework for businesses, not social systems. It is important to adopt the notion of intrinsic value as the goal for the business before implementing the SWAV.

The other aspect to the dark side is the negative perception of becoming a measurement-oriented organization. Some individuals think that measurement is intimately related to judgment of their performance. They connect this with negative connotations—that bad things will happen if a measurement system is put in place. This may be connected to a fear of failure. They think that a change in standards in the future may mean inability to perform to the new benchmarks. The reality is that people will need to become action-oriented and coordinate their activities around the creation of value. This brings us to organizational considerations.

Organizational Considerations

The purpose of this book is to align strategy with finance. A second level of alignment needs to occur to link these two disciplines, and that is the alignment between the valuation framework and the organization. This begins with an assessment of the value proposition for the individuals involved. If the individuals have something to lose, then expect resistance to the adoption of the framework on a corporate basis. If the staff has something to gain, they will welcome the process. Let's discuss perceived loss, as it will often create barriers to success.

The senior management team may feel a perceived loss of power resulting from the adoption of the SWAV. This perception is fueled by removing attributes of power advancement for managers. These attributes of power are:

- ❏ The number of direct reports
- ❏ The reporting structure
- ❏ The budget under management
- ❏ The ability to make decisions

Why are these attributes important? They are the drivers that determine further career advancement, organizational influence, and the money an executive can command in the marketplace. The number of reports and the size of budget under management are directly related to power. The higher up the organizational chart a person reports, the more power she has. If these attributes of power are diminished across the management team, then resistance to the SWAV will be high. Resistance may occur even with subtle changes such as creating a cross-reporting relationship with employees when forming an evaluation team. Evaluation of reengineering projects may meet resistance because they involve head count reduction. Another point of resistance may occur if operating unit budgets are tapped to fund the Strategic Alternative. These type of objections to the SWAV can be offset by having representation from every organizational level on the evaluation team.

Many managers feel that their decision-making ability is challenged by deployment of these techniques. Executives feel that if they need to use a specific framework as a justification of investment, their power as a manager is diminished. Many managers feel that their gut instincts are superior to quantitative justification. After using the framework they will find that they will get better results from using the method.

Another way of offsetting resistance from erosion

in the attributes of power is to link compensation to success of SAs. This involves tying compensation to performance-based metrics for a specific initiative.

In addition to the perception of erosion of power, executives may feel that past decisions will be perceived as wrong. Since managers did not have the more advanced tools to make decisions in the past, there is a possibility that the same decision would not be made using the SWAV. It is important to stress that the deployment of these techniques represents progress in the way decisions are made. Of course there have been bad decisions made in the past because management did not have the proper instrumentation to properly gauge value.

Process Issues

The SWAV needs to be supported by a strong process that involves cross-organizational integration. The salient process issues are listed below:

❏ *Senior management must support the SWAV.* Senior management must agree to the method and outcome of the approach. This means that they will accept the results of the process and not try to undermine it if it does not support their pet initiative.

❏ *The initiative team must be accountable.* A cross-functional team needs to be created for each SA. This team should consist of individuals who have deep enough knowledge about the particular organization from both analysis and execution. The entire team must be held responsible for the results of the analysis. We have seen situations where client team members would come to meetings with benefits estimates and present them without knowing the basis for the assumptions. The entire team needs to be held accountable for the integrity of the analysis.

❏ *Someone must be in charge.* The initiative team needs to be led by an individual who has the authority to make decisions about the direction of the analysis that will be accepted by senior managers. Putting someone in charge can be perceived as diminishing the power base of others on the management team, so this issue may create some difficulties.

❏ *Look-backs must be important.* It is critical that the results from the SAs are measured against forecasted value to determine if the assumptions made in the SWAV were valid. The process and the framework need to be refined over time to be indicative of current business conditions. A library of assumptions should be created for the numerous initiative types. This will reduce the amount of time spent assessing an SA and improves the accuracy of the analysis. The implementation of the SA should be managed by the assumptions that are made in the SWAV.

In conclusion, this book presents a framework that can continually be improved. I welcome the addition of new analytical tools and practices to improve the SWAV. Business strategies need to adapt to changing economic and business conditions. Hence, assessment techniques need to be modified to accommodate those changes.

Bibliography

Brealy, Richard A., and Stewart C. Myers. *Principles of Corporate Finance*, 6th ed. New York: McGraw Hill, 2000.

Dielman, Terry E. *Applied Regression Analysis for Business and Economics*. Boston: PWS Kent, 1991.

Dunn & Bradstreet, http://www.dnb.com/local_home/local_home_US/.

Gates, Bill. *Business @ the Speed of Thought: Succeeding in the Digital Economy*. New York: Warner Business Books, 1999.

Jones, Charles, P. *Investments: Analysis and Management,* 7th ed. New York: Wiley & Sons, 2000, p. 198.

Ibid. *Investments: Analysis and Interpretation*. New York: John Wiley & Sons, 2000, p. 183.

Kaplan, Robert S., and David P. Norton. *The Balanced Scorecard: Translating Strategy into Action*. Boston: Harvard Business School Press, 1996, p. 61.

Lingle, John, H., and William Schienman. "From Balanced Scorecard to Strategic Gauges: Is It Worth It?" *Management Review*, March 1996, v85, n3, p. 56.

Merriam Webster's Collegiate Dictionary, 10th ed., 1999.

McKinsey & Company, Inc., Copeland, Tom, Tim Koller, and Jack Murrin. *Valuation: Measuring and Managing the Value of Companies,* 3rd ed. New York: John Wiley & Sons, 2000, p. 77.

Michael F. Corbett & Associates, Ltd. "Outsourcing Failures?" http://www.firmbuilder.com/articles/19/48/388/.

Porter, Michael, E. *Competitive Strategy: Techniques for Analyzing Industries and Competitors.* Boston: Harvard Business School Press, 1987.

The Federal Reserve Bulletin on "Profits and balance sheet developments at U.S. commercial banks in 1998." U.S. Department of Commerce, Bureau of Economic Analysis.

Index